T0358692

Writing Successful Grant Proposals

TEACHING WRITING

Volume 3

Series Editor

Patricia Leavy
USA

International Editorial Board

Liza Ann Acosta, *North Park University, USA*
Sandra L. Faulkner, *Bowling Green State University, USA*
Lee Gutkind, *Arizona State University, USA*
Anne Harris, *Monash University, Australia*
Yvonna S. Lincoln, *Texas A&M University, USA*
David Manderson, *University of West Scotland, UK*
Ronald Pelias, *Southern Illinois University, USA*
Rita Rud, *Washington State University, USA*
Candace Stout, *The Ohio State University, USA*
Jonathan Wyatt, *The University of Edinburgh, UK*

Scope

The *Teaching Writing* series publishes concise instructional writing guides. Series books each focus on a different subject area, discipline or type of writing. The books are intended to be used in undergraduate and graduate courses across the disciplines and can also be read by individual researchers or students engaged in thesis work.

Series authors must have a demonstrated publishing record and must hold a PhD, MFA or the equivalent. Please email queries to the series editor at pleavy7@aol.com

Writing Successful Grant Proposals

Ellen W. Gorsevski

SENSE PUBLISHERS
ROTTERDAM/BOSTON/TAIPEI

A C.I.P. record for this book is available from the Library of Congress.

ISBN: 978-94-6300-388-9 (paperback)
ISBN: 978-94-6300-389-6 (hardback)
ISBN: 978-94-6300-390-2 (e-book)

Published by: Sense Publishers,
P.O. Box 21858,
3001 AW Rotterdam,
The Netherlands
https://www.sensepublishers.com/

All chapters in this book have undergone peer review.

Printed on acid-free paper

All Rights Reserved © 2016 Sense Publishers

No part of this work may be reproduced, stored in a retrieval system, or transmitted in any form or by any means, electronic, mechanical, photocopying, microfilming, recording or otherwise, without written permission from the Publisher, with the exception of any material supplied specifically for the purpose of being entered and executed on a computer system, for exclusive use by the purchaser of the work.

PRAISE FOR
WRITING SUCCESSFUL GRANT PROPOSALS

"This little book gets quickly to the important points. Even better, Dr. Gorsevski has been around the grant-writing block a few times herself. She's giving honest answers and pragmatic advice. This is all the stuff you really need to know!"
– Dale Cyphert, Ph.D., Associate Professor of Management, College of Business Administration, University of Northern Iowa

"Great! It will be very helpful to countless academics. I have been looking for a short, targeted grant-writing book [like this] all my academic life, because successful grant-writing keeps academic careers and institutions alive. The volume is encouraging, fact-filled (e.g., making your proposal stand out through images, sounds, and media), and resource-rich (e.g., finding grant opportunities). It comprehensively walks readers through the entire grant-writing process. Unlike most books on grant-writing, this one is lively, witty, and even anxiety-reducing, making first-time and veteran grant-writers more eager to take on the task. The last chapter, a newsworthy feature, explains what to do after the grant has been won, e.g., using polite immodesty, use-or-lose budgeting, and marketing of successes. I highly recommend this book and will tell all my colleagues about it."
– Rebecca L. Oxford, Ph.D., Professor Emerita, Distinguished Scholar-Teacher, University of Maryland and author of *The Language of Peace: Communicating to Create Harmony*

"Finally! A savvy book on grants that speaks to large social concerns of peace, environment, justice and multiple audiences. Gorsevski's book is a much needed resource for agency, academic and volunteer leaders alike regarding the do's and don'ts of dealing with diverse donors and RFPs."
– George A. Lopez, Hesburgh Professor of Peace Studies Emeritus, University of Notre Dame, and former Vice-President of the US Institute of Peace

"Dr. Gorsevski offers an excellent guide into the life of writing grants. Grant writing tools are critical instruments to the infrastructure of nonprofits and this book is a great asset. Her explanation of what a grant is offers step-by-step instructions for every stage of the grant process, which she makes clear is not without challenges. For beginner grant writers to the experienced writer, this book is a must have that ensures the reader leaves nothing to chance when taking on the large task of writing a grant. I highly recommend it."
– Catherine Wyatt-Morley, Founder and Chief Executive Officer, Women On Maintaining Education and Nutrition, Nashville, TN

TABLE OF CONTENTS

PREFACE

As was often the case with proposals work, our firm's engineers had made some late-hour changes. I was revising and double-checking the proposal right up until the last minute.

Hyperventilating, I made the two copies of the proposal on the persnickety copy machine. It was 1:45 in the afternoon. I had to make it to the FedEx delivery drop by 2 p.m. Copies done, I placed them one by one into the hole-puncher for the comb style binding. Once the holes (which were not round, but rather were long, narrow rectangles) were punched, next I had to slide each of the stacks of paper into the comb binder insert machine. The hand-cranked machine would usually make the comb miss a page or two, which then had to be fixed manually. It was 1:50 p.m. Damn-it! I couldn't miss that FedEx or my job was on the line. This project proposal was worth hundreds of thousands of dollars in business to my company. If awarded, the project would pay all of our company's employee salaries, nationwide.

By 1:53 p.m. I was sliding the two completed masterpieces into the pre-addressed FedEx shipping envelope. I grabbed my purse, car keys, and the package and ran down the stairs, almost twisting my ankle at the stairwell. Stupid high heels! Reaching my car, it was 1:55 p.m. It usually took ten minutes to get across town to the FedEx drop. I weaved through downtown traffic, barely stopping at stop signs to look, and then gunning the engine. As I pulled into the parking lot of the drop station, to my dismay I saw the FedEx truck driver getting into the truck and starting his engine. He had already finished his pick-up from the drop box! There was only one thing to do.

I drove right up in front of the huge truck and blocked it with my tiny car so he couldn't drive away. Furious, he got out, hollering, "Hey Lady! What the ...?" He gestured with both his hands and arms as if shooing away a big fly, saying, "Move your car out of my way!"

"Please! Wait!" I implored. "Please take this package, it's got to go out today," I said breathlessly, lurching out from behind the driver's seat with my package.

"Fine!" he retorted, clearly irritated. Grabbing the package from my trembling hands, he added, "Just this once. But don't you ever try this stunt again!"

It was 1993, and I was working as a full-time proposal writer for a small construction management company. The company had three offices, one branch was in Washington, D.C., where I was initially hired, the main headquarters in Durham, North Carolina, and a west coast office in California, somewhere beyond greater Los Angeles. It was my job to write proposals to local city, state, and federal government entities to garner projects for our company. Usually marketers or engineers would locate the call for a grant from local listings of requests for proposals (RFPs), hand it over to me, and then I'd work my magic. I spent some time on the phone, asking engineers how things worked, or sometimes asking them to write a few paragraphs about technical aspects of projects that only they would know.

I worked typically six days a week. During frequent deadline weeks, I would work every day from seven in the morning until midnight. Most days, I barely had time to eat; I was gaunt and thoroughly exhausted. I had ulcers. I drank coffee all the time, which did not sufficiently keep me awake but only made me more anxious.

I am not certain if it was this moment of crisis in front of the FedEx truck when I decided to quit, or some of the many other awful, stressful hours I spent in that job. But I left that company shortly thereafter, and went on to earn a Master's degree in Speech Communication. The required course work in the excellent program at Oregon State University included classes on the ancient art form that had become a contemporary science of *rhetoric*, which to my amazement I realized I had been practicing already as a proposal writer. I learned that rhetorical theory and practice was a mainstay for politicians, diplomats, corporate heads, and other movers and shakers.

As a proposal writer, I had been just doing persuasive writing instinctively, intuitively, but without the valuable theoretical base of knowledge about persuasion as a roadmap, which my graduate coursework was now providing. After completing my Master's degree, I went on to earn a doctorate at Penn State University. Throughout my graduate school years, I found the hands-on experience and work ethic I'd developed during my early technical editing and proposal writing jobs really came in handy.

Following graduate school, as a budding academic, I continued to do more grant proposal writing, with some success, which I have been fortunate enough to continue to this day. I have found that when I combine my public and private sector experiences, skills, and knowledge, I can prove to be a rather formidable grant proposal writer.

Locating funders, researching projects, and writing, organizing, and submitting grant proposals can be a challenging process. Nowadays the old copy machine battle and tedious struggle with the comb binder for a paper proposal has been in most cases replaced with endless online, web-based submittal forms, which inevitably crash the second you start to click on the 'Submit' button, thus losing all your information and necessitating a redoing of *all* the online forms. With proposals, it seems, there are few short-cuts.

Fortunately, now as a professor, I am no longer in a completely "soft money" (meaning 100 percent self-funded) position that necessitates the teeth grinding, ulcer-inducing nightmare of having to write, assemble, and submit grant proposals all the time. I do, however, still write small grant proposals periodically so as to help fund my research projects.

This wee guidebook is designed to help others with what I have learned about writing successful grant proposals. There are some things savvy proposal writers can do to make their projects attractive to prospective funders. This book may not necessarily be able to reduce all of the stress that comes with writing grant proposals, nor can any reputable person or book or weekend seminar guarantee a successful outcome for all proposals, many of which are subject to the vagaries of politics and economic boom and bust cycles. But this book does assist with demystifying grant proposal development, which can often seem like, and occasionally prove to be, a quite complicated and intimidating process.

In the chapters which follow, I share with readers some effective strategies for writing the proposal, and also for staying on-task and getting the project you proposed completed on time, and within the financial limits listed on the proposal's budget list. And since some grant agencies still occasionally call for a paper copy to be sent by old fashioned postal mail or a shipping service, try not to vex the driver of the delivery truck.

ACKNOWLEDGEMENTS

There are many opportunities for academics to write books these days, but few of these books ever wind up being useful in what is often referred to as 'the real world,' or, to update in gender-neutral terms the old saw from country and western music, the 'working person's Ph.D.' Having both kinds of career experience, in which much time was spent writing grant proposals, I have learned many of the tips I have provided here by doing enough gophering, which led to collaborating, then to leading, and now, to a measure of mastery that merits sharing.

Because this rare little book was enabled to come into being as a guide that would be useful in many a working person's realms, I would like to thank Patricia Leavy and Peter de Liefde (Sense Publishers) for their expansive vision and for giving me the chance to write it. I would also like to thank Shalen Lowell and Jolanda Karada for able assistance with formatting and other book production guidance.

Much gratitude goes to my family and friends for granting me extra hermit time at work to get this weighty wee tome written.

WRITING GRANTS THAT SUCCEED

Harnessing the Power of Rhetorical Theory and Practice

There are many long-winded grant writing books out there that go into excruciating detail about how to research, write, assemble, and submit a successful grant. Even *Grant Writing for Dummies* is nearly 300 pages long! I do not attempt to duplicate that level of detail in this little handbook.

Indeed, to be transparent from the start, I must delineate for whom this book is written and for whom it is not written. This book is mainly designed for proposal writers in the arts and humanities. It is primarily for single authored projects, and for lesser amounts of money. Most of my grants are in the range of up to $1,000 to about $5,000 or less. That is the kind of small change I am talking about. But remember, small change, when saved and added up, can cumulatively yield great long-range fiduciary and career success.

Certainly the tips that follow in this book could potentially be used to write grant proposals seeking funds in the six-figure range, and perhaps even more. But my heart beats and flutters for the small but worthy projects that typically do not win large suitcases of money. In an age of cold statistics, cyber-existence, electronic gadgets, and space-age violence, I seek to help those whose creative themes and peaceful projects can be sustained by modest funds that keep the arts and humanities alive.

This book is not primarily for giant teams of scientific researchers seeking to clone the best and fastest race horse by acquiring many millions of dollars in private-sector funding of oil-rich Texas entrepreneurs, nor is it intended for scientists seeking to grab millions of bucks to grow giant sequoia trees out of petri dishes, nor is it crafted for purveyors of military hardware and software who seek billions of dollars in funding by the federal government to enhance military-grade toilet seats or radar-invisible panelling on fighter jet wings and unpiloted drones.

Instead, this book is for the lone researcher, mainly in the humanities. It will probably be most useful to scholars who work with just themselves, but with no more than very small groups of people, such as two- or three-person teams of researchers. In short, I use my more than 20 years of experience writing successful grants to provide a less daunting introduction and overview of the basic components of a successful grant proposal. I sketch and advise how to get the writing done. I also discuss how to handle completing the work that you promise to your granting agency that you will accomplish on time and within the budget you estimated.

With brief but concise handbooks that have stood the test of time as role models, this little tome is designed to provide a clear, simplified entry point into the daunting world of grant writing. For my purposes in this handbook on how to write grants that succeed, I follow the path of old standby's of vigorous, high quality writing that are paragons of brevity and wisdom, such as William Strunk and E. B. White's *Elements of Style* (1979), or for rhetorical theory, Arthur Quinn's *Figures of Speech: 60 Ways to Turn a Phrase* (1982). With these timeless and refreshingly brief paragons in mind, this grants writing book condenses what I view are the most useful yet frustratingly ineffable aspects of successful grant writing.

In a nutshell, writing grants that succeed in garnering a monetary award involves four core skills: writing well, being persuasive, and being organized and diligent. As Quinn (1982) puts it, "Writing is not like chemical engineering. We shouldn't learn the figures of speech the way we learn the periodic table of elements… Learning about the figures of speech … [is more] like learning how to model clay" (p. 2). Similarly, learning how to write high quality grants is more like an artful exercise, such as *yoga* or *tai chi*, which one may begin to attempt rather clumsily, but if one keeps at it, with practice, one can become quite versatile and perhaps even master the art form.

Grants are the great leveller. It is not always the most popular person, nor the handsomest, nor the highest paid, who always lands the grant. Just as *yoga* or *tai chi* as both art forms and exercises can be practiced and done well by a portly senior citizen with arthritic joints, so too can grants writing be done well by the independent humanities proposal writer who is not at a Research I institution in higher education. It is not the individual grant writer's glowing stature of being ensconced in an endowed professorship in the ivory tower that necessarily will attract grant funding, nor is always the youthful, willowy selfie-taker that may have the proper *yoga* form and movement: she may be too distracted by her fancy pants that recharge her phone while she does a crooked downward dog to notice that the 80-year old lady to her right is striking the perfect pose. So, it is the writer who is able to argue persuasively and straightforwardly to a group of variously bored, tired, and often grumpy grants reviewers. Grants reviewers are people who are frequently tired and overworked. So what will capture and sustain their attention?

What distinguishes the successful grant writer from her competitors is that her grant proposal *speaks* to the exhausted reviewer, rousing him or her from torpor. Meanwhile, the 49 other dull proposals that the reviewers have in the stacks on their desks (yes, there are plenty of old-school paper readers still out there), or cluttering up their laptops' hard drives, or their employer's electronic 'cloud,' are only soporific means to send them off on their next Starbucks run. How does a grant writer transform the seemingly boring and technical genre of proposal writing into an opera that sings, arousing even the most lethargic of readers and audience members to a state of agreeable acceptance, if not outright rapture? The answer to that requires some introductory discussion of an ancient theory, art form and exercise that is as old and well-practiced as *yoga* or *tai chi*: that art form and exercise is called *rhetoric*.

RHETORIC

What is Rhetoric?

Rhetoric is one of Aristotle's (1954) books that is often required reading for majors in degrees such as Communication or English. What Aristotle attempted to do was to explain the process of persuading audiences to agree with a speaker or writer. It sounds quite simple, but rhetoric can be a very difficult art form because, like *yoga* or *tai chi*, it requires a lot of practice. Aristotle, along with hundreds of other great and little known scholars alike from wisdom traditions worldwide, reminds us that while 'rhetoric' can certainly mean its first dictionary definition that we today associate with the term, which is usually something like 'BS' or 'empty fluff,' rhetoric means the artful and seductive use of language, including its ordering, organization and movement, to win over someone else. Using rhetoric denotes *convincing people to agree with your desires* to accomplish a task or to ponder new perspectives. Therefore, if you are writing a grant to, say, study the frescos in a cave in a war-torn part of the world, you must persuade your potential, prospective funders to agree that doing so would be a worthwhile endeavour.

...so what does rhetoric have to do with successful grant writing?

The individual grant reviewer who decides your proposal is worthwhile might not want to spend her life looking at frescos, and certainly not to schlep along with you through active minefields to get to the cave in question, but you have, through rhetoric, given the reviewer the imagination to see that, nonetheless, this would be a worthwhile activity. The reviewer, then, need not agree with your lifestyle, nor your perspective, nor even your politics. The reviewer simply needs to agree that such actions are potentially useful in some objective sense. Hence understanding and using rhetoric is instrumental to winning that reviewer over to deciding to fund your grant.

Take the early example of an iconic critical thinker gauging rhetoric as functioning like cultural and political glue to a nation-state. For Aristotle, rhetoric is "a faculty [or ability or skill, depending on the translation from Greek] for observing in any given case all the available means of persuasion." In other words, socio-linguistic practitioners who are versant in rhetoric are like the MacGyvers of language. Instead of taking a toothpick and using it to dig his way out of quicksand like MacGyver might, or Bear Grylls' inevitable rope to get Kate Hudson to rappel down a steep cliff, the successful grant writer uses words to capture and sustain the attention, and more importantly, the purse, of the institution or grant agency that funds the project the proposal writer seeks to do.

Likewise with Aristotle's many international compatriots in obsessing over the art and science of rhetoric as an erudite person's skill in persuasion, such as Islamic scholar Ibn Rushd (Borrowman, 2008; Clark, 2007), or China's sage Confucius (Ding, 2007), valuing lucid communication that arouses readers and audiences' imaginations and, importantly, the urge to elicit agreement, is an archetypal preoccupation of human kind. Rhetoric, then, is quite certainly *not* fluff: rhetoric is indeed a goodly part of the substance that makes for winning grant proposals.

For Ibn Rushd, a scholar who studied and translated Aristotle's *Rhetoric* for Islamic audiences, the art and exercise of *al-bayan* (clarity) and *al-badi* (metaphors and figures of speech) were rhetorical means to fostering messages of social uplift, in ways such as creating beautiful poetry for cultural cohesion and for fostering morality, everyone could appreciate and apply skilful uses of language (Borrowman, 2008; Merriam, 1974). Similarly, for wide-ranging walks of life of peasants to courtesans to emperors, Confucius understood that rhetoric combining word and deed was the key to rising from lowly social status, to maintaining efficient organizational communication, to aptly performing kingly tasks of being a wise and fair ruler (Ding, 2007; You, 2006).

For today's proposal writer seeking a grant from organizations both large and small, an awareness of rhetoric as a both ancient and contemporary form of art and practice is essential. Consider rhetoric as the international and intercultural impetus to communicate clearly and beautifully, which takes practice. Rhetoric entails an endless learning curve that is global in its scope. Crucially for successful grant writing, recognizing the reality that many of today's grants-giving organizations are both international and intercultural (even when they might not seem like it), is also a vital skill. Successful writers of grant proposals understand how to reach audiences, draw them in, and keep them cosseted in a message that resonates with a richness and diversity reflective of multifaceted readers, listeners as multiethnic, multiracial, multilingual, and multinational grants donors. Just as rhetoric for the ancients was a knowledge base and skills set for worldly statesmen, so, too, today is rhetoric in theory and practice necessary for prosperous lawyers, thriving politicians, diplomats, and popular speech writers (Fieler, 2015).

Returning to the point of this book, rhetoric is a critical skill to have for thriving academics and staffers at small, non-profit organizations and nongovernmental organizations (NGOs) who must write successful grant proposals in order to survive and flourish. As federal and state dollars are increasingly being cut from higher education and from not-for-profit social agencies, being able to write persuasive grant proposals to win funding awards from granting agencies is a necessary skills set. For the independent humanities scholar seeking to fund dissertation research on the dogs and cats of great writers like Shakespeare, to the scrappy, skeleton-crew-staffed non-profit organization that is attempting to press for sane, reasonable gun policies in a society awash in semi-automatic weapons used not on backwoods deer nor battlefields but in movie theatres or schools to mow down innocent bystanders, writing well and writing persuasively can enable projects to get funded.

In short, for aspiring grant writers, grasping rhetoric and using it adroitly in developing proposals helps to get projects funded. A basic, working knowledge of rhetoric as a theory, art form, and form of exercise is particularly advantageous to seeking, developing and gaining grant funding for the kind of small, sometimes arcane, quirky projects that liberal arts researchers, humanities scholars and social work and progressive organizations often undertake. Rhetoric, when applied judiciously in grant narratives, enables the unsung and underfunded projects to get funded: rhetoric helps underdogs to fly.

REFERENCES

Aristotle. (1954). *Rhetoric* (W. Rhys Roberts, Trans.). New York, NY: Random House.

Borrowman, S. (2008). The islamization of "rhetoric": Ibn Rushd and the reintroduction of Aristotle into medieval Europe. *Rhetoric Review, 27*(4), 341–360.

Clark, C. L. (2007). Aristotle and Averroes: The influences of Aristotle's Arabic commentator upon western European and Arabic rhetoric. *Review of Communication, 7*(4), 369–387.

Ding, H. (2007). Confucius's virtue-centered rhetoric: A case study of mixed research methods in comparative rhetoric. *Rhetoric Review, 26*(2), 142–159. doi:10.1080/07350190701313040

Fieler, B. (2015, June 19). Turning to a ghostwriter for a personal toast. *The New York Times*. Retrieved from http://www.nytimes.com/2015/06/21/style/toast-whisperers-ghostwriters-personal-speeches.html?_r=0

Merriam, A. H. (1974). Rhetoric and the Islamic tradition. *Today's Speech, 22*(1), 43–44.

Quinn, A. (1982). *Figures of speech: 60 ways to turn a phrase*. Salt Lake City, UT: A Peregrin Smith Book.

Strunk, W., Jr., & White, E. B. (1979). *The elements of style* (3rd ed.). New York, NY: Macmillan.

You, X. (2006). The way, multimodality of ritual symbols, and social change: Reading Confucius's analects as a rhetoric. *Rhetoric Society Quarterly, 36*(4), 425–448. doi:10.1080/02773940600868028

CHAPTER 1

WHAT IS A GRANT PROPOSAL?

And Where Do I Find Grants to Apply for?

INTRODUCTION

Grant proposal writing is a survival skill that can heighten job security and professional opportunities in times of economic upheaval. For many career paths in the non-profit sector, including academia, think tanks, small non-profit organizations, writing grant proposals can be anything along the spectrum from an occasional annoyance to an all-consuming, overtime-inducing preoccupation. But what exactly is a grant? What is a proposal? And how are these two things related?

A grant is typically an allotment of funds that an organization that is tasked with disbursing those funds to awardees it sees as worthy individuals, teams or entities, such as those noted above, to accomplish a specific project. Sometimes grants will include non-monetary aspects as well, such as offering so called 'in-kind' support. For instance, there may be pre-paid lodging for a writer-in-residence post at a prestigious university or think tank. So while enticing, it is not always the large monetary grant that will best support a specific project. Sometimes a smaller grant may yield benefits that may feature a monetary quality, such as lodging, but other benefits may accrue, too. There may be prestige associated with a given grant, or perhaps there will be professional networking opportunities linked to a grant, and so forth. Grant awards, like scuba diving gear or prom dresses, can be wildly different yet still useful in being tailor-made to the purposes of the project you are proposing to do.

In the public sector, there are city, county, state and federal government grants to accomplish small projects such as planting flowers along traffic medians dividing roads, or installing flower baskets along Main Street of a town, or large projects such as developing a space craft that can fly to Mars and bring back data about its potential for habitable life on that famous red planetary neighbour of earth. In short, a grant can be as small or large as the project envisioned by the agency that is offering the funds to prospective experts of all kinds and backgrounds to accomplish specific tasks.

What is a proposal? A proposal is a written plan offering to conduct the type of work that is requested by the agency offering the funds, whether that project is flower planting or Mars voyaging, or book writing or documentary film-making.

A proposal is a document that essentially does three things. First, the proposal states who you are and why you are qualified to plant flowers or build spaceships or write books or make cinematic masterpieces. Second, the proposal outlines your step-by-step plan to get the work done and the time-frame in which you promise to complete the work. Third, the proposal usually requires a detailed budget, listing on a grid or spreadsheet each aspect of the work that you will do along with its associated cost. For example, if you are a geologist who needs to study moon rocks in order to figure out how your spaceship to Mars will gather rock samples, you might include in your proposal's budget items like travel costs. Travel costs entail aspects you would like for the grant to pay for, such as hotel and airfare, for a visit to NASA's Lyndon B. Johnson Space Center in Houston, Texas to study the earth's largest collection of moon rocks (Atkinson, 2009; Space Center, 2015).

To be able to write a successful grant means that first you must have a good idea. If creativity does not come naturally for you, it may surprise you to learn that grant writers need not be born creative, but effective grant writers do need to practice a lot to build their ability to be innovative. Take, for instance, Apple computer's grammatically questionable but brilliant slogan (Evans, 2015), "Think different."[1] Just like a body-builder builds muscle: with endless repetition of attempts to articulate a state of simultaneous difference and high quality, budding grant writers can improve their ability to communicate with excellence.

Grant writers who are successful must come up with a great idea, and then commit that idea to writing in a stringent form of technical and professional writing that conforms to the request for proposal (RFP), which is also sometimes referred to as the call for grant applications. RFPs and calls for grants can be as rigid in form as poets' uses of *haiku* or the iambic pentameter. Grant writing or proposal writing is highly structured and well organized. Truly successful proposal write-ups add extra elements of originality and uniqueness, which help to set them apart. But we will return to discussing tips for inventiveness in Chapter 3. For now, let's begin with the basics.

HOW TO FIND GRANTS TO WRITE PROPOSALS FOR

Seek and Ye Shall Write

Before grant writers can commit words to the page to plug their projects that they seek to be funded, they must first locate funders which are seeking to fund projects. Where are these elusive funders?

In a world of endless and seemingly ever heightening competition, it might appear to be hopeless to try to get a grant funded to study the pet project of, say, a mom who is a peacebuilding tree hugger in a developing nation. But Wangari Maathai, a Kenyan mother and university professor who would later become the first ever environmentalist to be awarded a Nobel Peace prize, found small, international funders—far away in Norway—to help her initiate what would evolve into what is today the Green Belt Movement (GBM). Presently the GBM is a powerful international non-profit organization and educational, activist movement to reverse the negative effects of interrelated problems of topsoil loss, desertification, and climate change by having local people do a simple thing: plant tree saplings. Splendid ideas remain just that until they find a person or organization to help bring the notions to fruition with the injection of a reasonable amount of cash.

For virtually every kind of project, there is a funder out there waiting to give monetary backing and other kinds of invaluable support, such as assistance with marketing and promotion, training, or mentoring. Although the avenues for funding described here below are far from exhaustive, they constitute a good start to helping aspiring grant writers to locate grant agencies that offer RFPs and calls for applications for a host of grant proposals. There are one-time, periodic, or well-endowed perennial funds to annually award different worthwhile projects. Seek and ye shall write!

What Is the Best Way to Get Started Looking for Grants?

Beyond the avenues discussed here below, there is above all, one incredibly useful place to start. Begin your grants journey at your local town, city or nearby university library's information desk.

Librarians get a bum rap. Many people think of libraries too often as repositories of books, and librarians as nerdy relics of a bygone era, but that is a great misconception. While adept at finding books, today's librarians are actually just as knowledgeable in how to sort through the immense overloads of information and misinformation that exists in today's electronic world, where everyone has a blog, and many an uninformed opinion. Most qualified

3

librarians can help direct you how to sift judiciously through the vast world of grants listings online, in books or in periodicals. Think of your librarian as your efficient and loyal *aide-de-camp* in the process of sorting the useful from the bogus venues for grants. Even if you do not work for an academic institution, as a state resident and taxpayer most citizens will have access to the best state university libraries and librarians' expertise, which are often within a reasonable driving distance away, and well worth the visit. If you are a non-resident or international visitor or scholar, usually there are work-arounds that will nonetheless enable you to use high quality state university library services. Graduate students and international faculty have access to all the same wide variety of library and research assistance support as anyone else, so be sure you seek and get all the help that is available to you.

After reading this chapter, which should give you a good idea of what kinds of grants might fit your base of interests, skills and experience, go to your nearest library. Equipped with questions that occur to you, and which you note as you read, ask the librarian for help in pinpointing sources of funding and calls for grants in your research area or domain of professional practice.

If you work for an academic institution or established organization, there may be one or more full time grants support staffers who can assist you as well with the many stages and phases of grant proposal development and production and submission. Also talk to experienced professionals who have done grant proposal writing and submissions in your field and in your area of expertise for advice and, if possible, proofreading and revising help. We will talk more about the nuts and bolts of writing grant proposals in Chapters 2 and 3, but for now let's focus on how to get started.

Networking: Nurture Personal and Professional Connections

It may be considered common sense, but it is important to nurture personal and professional connections because you never know who might offer you that lucky break. Asking someone interesting to join you for a cup of coffee or tea can usually yield the moral support you need, and occasionally the mention of an opportunity that you had not yet before considered. Also, attending professional workshops, seminars, conferences and classes may sometimes seem like a superfluous expense. However, by meeting up with like-minded professionals, you will be making a fruitful investment in your work.

Martha Stewart, one of the most successful women corporate heads and mavens of all things domestic, has said she actually finds it difficult to date people because she always starts to talk business and her date ends up being like another meeting leading to a business venture. So while it is perhaps not advisable to go to the extreme of not being able to take a break from your professional side, it is crucial for your life and your career to talk to other people. Yes, even for introverts and ambiverts, putting your cell phone on airplane mode, setting aside your laptop, and talking to people in person is crucial for most careers, and this is particularly so for aspiring grant proposal writers.

To be sure, Skype or phone conversations can be helpful, but there is nothing that can replace the potential for person-to-person positive energy transfer that can happen in the magic of a physically emplaced moment with other smart people around you, talking to you, and you with them. Cesar Millan, a successful 'dog whisperer,' often characterizes what he does not as dog training, but as people training. Millan describes his work in reshaping people's energy in this way:

> Energy is what I call beingness; it is who and what you are in every moment. Dogs don't know each other by name, but by the energy they project and the activities they share. They know humans in the same way. As humans, we too are communicating with energy – whether we realize it or not. (Millan, 2015)

Sharing and gaining energy from other people may sound a bit 'woo-woo' or New Age-y, but for productive networking, projecting and commingling positive energy is a necessary activity. Networking takes practice. Sharing positive, productive energy is like skiing or playing tennis or basketball with someone who is better than you—you can learn and improve yourself by watching their expertise in action, and by mimicking their moves. Surrounding yourself as a grant writer with others who have gone before you, and who have written successful proposals, can be quite helpful.

Andrew Carnegie had his 'Brain Trust,' a group of well-educated and experienced advisors who helped him become and to remain one of the wealthiest industrialists of his day. Likewise, by talking to people in your personal and professional life about your interests and goals, you can set in motion an infrastructure of support. Wise and successful proposal writers often get advice, input, and even opportunities that enrich their ability to seek, develop, write, and garner a grant in their chosen areas of work.

Joining professional organizations is a great way to find out what grant opportunities are being listed all the time. Professional associations usually come with old timey newsletters on paper as well as email-based listserves, which periodically offer listings of calls, invitations and RFPs to apply for. National and international associations exist in most fields of work and study, and offer annual conventions and informative workshops, among other opportunities to network with fellow practitioners in your field.

So get out there. Sign up for a grant writing workshop. Join a professional association. Find mentors. Approach that successful person in your field after their conference presentation and introduce yourself. Successful proposal writers seek out other productive people to gain access to wise suggestions, to be in the loop in terms of ever arising opportunities, and to be able to gather and consider different perspectives.

Online Venues: Web Sites and Crowdsourcing

Using the web today and social media is simply an evolving extension of using traditional personal networks of friends and colleagues to seek to garner funding support for proposed projects. All manner of ideas and products, some worthy and others less so, get advertised and awarded through Internet venues.

Crowdsourcing is simply taking the old fashioned request of a friend or prospective business partner, which used to happen primarily in person, or secondarily by letter or telephone, and placing the proposed project onto a website forum where it can be viewed publically, assessed for its merit, and ideally, funded by people who are interested in the project (Howe, 2006). Look to the ample array of web based venues, such as Crowdsourcing.org, for ideas and platforms through which project funding can be sought.

Newspapers

Although competitive newspapers have increasingly been moving their content away from paper form and into online formats, in cities of all sizes nationwide, many old fashioned newspapers, which are printed on paper and sold at newsstands, surprisingly remain a useful source of information about possible opportunities for grant proposals and funding.

Granted, it may seem counterintuitive to younger generations with many millions of dollars in spending power on the Web daily and on special events such as the much ballyhooed Cyber Monday, but the majority of Americans and citizens in many nations worldwide continue to read newspapers on paper. Newspapers still matter, even as the news media are straddling paper and cyber formats.

With America's population in particular increasingly an older demographic, and with many well-backed funders, members of boards of trustees in all kinds of companies and institutions usually maintain a lot of silver haired persons on board. These active and empowered older people, aged 65 and over, still read newspapers by the millions. People are also waiting to retire until later years than prior generations, so chances are, your grant proposal could be sought after, advertised, reviewed, and possibly funded by someone who still values and uses newspapers.

Keeping up to speed on the daily news from newspapers, which yield listings of public requests for proposals, is one way to find out what is going on, what problems may need attention and redress, and what kinds of projects may be funded. From the small town local-yokel's newspaper to the *International Herald Tribune*, reading and using newspapers remains a useful habit for enterprising proposal writers.

Public Sector: Governmental Agencies

Governmentally sponsored grants abound, from grants offered by the smallest little burg or village to grants from large, international consortiums of collaborating governments. Government grants are called for all the time. Government grants can prove to be especially challenging to apply for because they typically have extensive, complicated online submissions processes and stringent eligibility criteria.

That said, well written proposals to governments are worthwhile to seek out and to undertake because the work they do can help to create awareness and to foster change. Also, once a grants seeker has attained a government award and delivered the promised work, governments tend to be reliable repeat funders, looking to fund those individuals and groups who have proven they can do the work that was promised.

International. While the world today certainly falls short of reaching any perfect kind of global governance, the closest thing to a collaborative world government would be organizations comprised of powerful international governments, such as the United Nations or the G8, which represent—albeit imperfectly—generally agreed upon criteria for issues such as international trade or treatment of prisoners of war, human rights, and limits on pollution as well as norms for addressing climate change. The United Nations (U.N.), through its many branches, offers international and transnational opportunities for proposing and conducting funded work or study.

7

For instance, a specialist in Mediterranean maritime trade, who speaks fluent Modern Standard Arabic, might look into which calls or invitations to bid (ITB) of the U.N.'s Economic and Social Commission for Western Asia (ESCWA) relate to a maritime area of expertise. Another researcher who is interested in projects to study or restore revered antiquities could look for ITBs from the World Heritage Fund of the United Nations Educational, Scientific and Cultural Organization (UNESCO), which grants several million dollars for projects annually (UNESCO Funding, 2015). Yet another expert in journalism that creates awareness of and helps curb hate speech in a fragile, post-conflict society might seek ITBs with UNESCO's International Program for the Development of Communication (IPDC); the IPDC is set up to promote democratic practices within the mass media of small and developing nations (UNESCO-IPDC, 2015). There are many governmental organizations that collaborate across borders on shared problems, from socio-political issues like religious conflict to environmental issues such as desertification or flooding. Many of these internationally collaborative governmental organizations require the outsourcing of expertise, and calls for proposals for projects to assist with studying, managing, or preventing problems in cultural, social, political areas and in the natural environment.

National. At the national level, the U.S. federal government, like many countries' governments, solicits RFPs. The American federal government might, for example, fund a study on the reintroduction of wolves to Yellowstone National Park. The federal government is known for "analysis paralysis," in which issues are studied *ad nauseum* but too seldom is anything ever done about a given problem. For grant proposal seekers and writers, the government's collective proclivity to ponder constitutes a potential grant-making gold mine.

The federal government is comprised of people from all walks of life and a range of political and ideological beliefs, which foments an endless thirst for knowledge to justify political, economic and social actions. Proposal writers can slake that thirst. Proposal writers who are successful realize that the government's endless need to identify and to study problems creates a virtually perpetual cycle of calls for projects and a vast number of opportunities to research, develop and write proposals to meet the government's needs.

State. At the state level, state governments likewise face a host of problems that need to be tackled. For example, construction of a heavily traversed highway in San Antonio, Texas had to be stopped because a rare spider under protection of the Endangered Species Act was discovered in the roadbed, and had to be studied (5News.com, 2014). Lucky was the entomologist who had written a grant proposal to study that spider. Meanwhile, angry motorists, tired of traffic jams they hoped would be mitigated by the new highway, could be studied by sociologists with expertise in road rage. The American Society of Civil Engineers understands the problem of "red tape that drags projects out for many, many years" (Natale, quoted in 5News.com, 2014). Different states have different problems and levels of severity of red tape (Economist, 2014). Organizational efficiency experts could write proposals to help states improve their business climates by reducing red tape. The possibilities are extensive, if not endless, to propose and garner grants that help alleviate intractable problems.

City to county. At the city or county level, there are also funds to be sought, depending on the size and kind of town or region it is. Problems of sweatshop labor occurring in New York City will be different from that of Mobile, Alabama. As we will discuss in greater detail in Chapter 3, understanding and articulating the specific issues that are relevant to a given place will require an understanding, empathy, and discourse that resonates with the grant's reviewers in that milieu. City government budgets allow for all kinds of projects, but the size and scope of the project and the grant funds sought will be limited by issues such as the increasing problem of cities declaring bankruptcy, which have fewer funds to disburse than economically booming cities. A grant project funded by a bankrupt city, such as Detroit, Michigan, would likely be on a different scale from San Bernardino, California, which also filed for bankruptcy (Farmer, 2013; Plumer, 2013).

Other differences can apply to the process of seeking county-based grants. A primarily agricultural county in California would have different needs than an urban county, in terms of investment interests, employment, and demographics. A water shortage for a county that relies on tourism might have different causes and effects than drought conditions for a county that relies on agricultural crops such as almond trees (Rodriquez, 2015). Proposal writers need to be cognizant of such variations when searching for projects to be funded. Climate, both weather and political, affects the writing, reviewing and awarding of many grant proposals, including proposals for projects for city and county governments.

The possibilities of studying and addressing problems are extensive, and are often only limited by imagination. Government funding for grant projects, from local to national to international, can be capricious and subject to political changes of winds. However, funds are frequently available for savvy proposal writers who seek out government-funded grants of many different purposes and kinds.

Private Sector: Enterprises, Trusts, and Philanthropic Organizations

Trust 'doctor Phil'. No, not Oprah's counsellor, but Oprah Winfrey herself, who has topped lists of wealthy charitable donors for years. Not all generous benefactors, known as a philanthropists, necessarily need to be as wealthy as Lady O, but it is important to know that there are many donors of all income levels who may be interested in funding your project.

At this writing, the deficit of the U.S. government—one of the most powerful nations on earth—is about 18 trillion dollars and counting (U.S. Department of Treasury, 2015). Greece, renowned for its time honoured creations from democracy to the Doric column and tourism on gorgeous Greek islands, nearly defaulted on its loans, throwing world markets and nervous investors into a tizzy. The world over, any given government may be broke at least once, but there are still plenty of millionaires and billionaires out there. These people want to give their money to causes and projects they deem worthy. You, dear reader and aspiring grant proposal writer, could be just such a cause.

Many rich, private citizens of the world maintain philanthropic endeavours and favoured charitable organizations, which call for proposals to fund projects in both the arts and sciences. From King of Pop Michael Jackson, to record producer David Geffen, to filmmaker George Lucas of Star Wars fame, to Facebook's Mark Zuckerberg, many people with loads of cash to spare are looking to give some of it away (Bukszpan, 2015; Titcomb, 2014).

SUMMARY: WHERE TO START LOOKING FOR GRANTS

To recap this first chapter, if you wish to succeed in writing grant proposals that are competitive, you need to first locate reputable calls, invitations, or requests for proposals (RFPs). Public, or governmental agencies are looking to fund all sorts of projects, from studying noisy peacocks disturbing the peace in tiny townships, to immense federal government problems such as how to cut the mind-bogglingly enormous federal budget deficit. Private, or non-governmental sources of funding also exist, funded by entities such as trusts and wealthy individuals.

In order to locate viable RFPs, you need to get help. Based on what type of project you are seeking to get funded, you will narrow your search for grant agencies to those for which your skills and expertise fit. To gather intelligence about how to develop and write successful grant proposals, you need to surround yourself with a group of supportive and experienced individuals as your 'brain trust.' One of the most helpful persons to consult is a librarian. Other helpful people include mentors with experience in garnering grant awards. Networking and attending workshops and seminars on grants development can also be quite useful.

Listings of calls for proposals abound on the Internet, but there are also listings in local newspapers or trade periodicals.

NOTE

[1] The grammatically more common version of the slogan could have been "Think different*ly*." While exceptions to the use of 'different' as an adverb may exist, they are not common. Through uncommon grammar, Apple's marketing and advertising gurus in effect reiterated Apple products' purportedly unique qualities.

REFERENCES

5News. Endangered spider nearly triples cost for Texas highway construction. *5News.com*. Retrieved from http://5newsonline.com/2014/12/11/endangered-spider-nearly-triples-cost-for-texas-highway-project/

Atkinson, N. (2009). After 40 years moon rocks still revealing secrets. *UniverseToday.com*. Retrieved from http://www.universetoday.com/35404/after-40-years-moon-rocks-still-revealing-secrets/

Bukszpan, D. (2015). Meet today's philanthropists: They're super rich and super generous. *Fortune.com*. Retrieved from http://fortune.com/2015/03/19/philanthropists-billionaires-charity/

Davidson, M. (2013). *Moon rocks under the microscope. Molecular expressions*. Tallahassee, FL: Florida State University. Retrieved from http://micro.magnet.fsu.edu/publications/pages/rocks.html

Evans, J. (2015). The untold story behind Apple's 'Think Different' campaign. *ComputerWorld.com*. Retrieved from http://www.computerworld.com/article/2936344/apple-mac/the-untold-story-behind-apple-s-think-different-campaign.html

Farmer, L. (2013). San Bernardino becomes 3rd California city to get bankruptcy protection. *Governing*. Retrieved from http://www.governing.com/blogs/view/gov-judge-awards-san-bernardino-bankruptcy-protection.html

Howe, J. (2006). The rise of crowdsourcing. *Wired Magazine, 14.6*. Retrieved from http://archive.wired.com/wired/archive/14.06/crowds.html

Millan, C. (2015). How to be calm and assertive. *Cesar's Way* [blog]. Retrieved from http://www.cesarsway.com/dog-psychology/pack-leader/how-to-be-calm-and-assertive

Plumer, B. (2013). Detroit isn't alone. The U.S. cities that have gone bankrupt, in one map. *The Washington Post.* Retrieved from http://www.washingtonpost.com/ news/wonkblog/wp/2013/07/18/detroit-isnt-alone-the-u-s-cities-that-have-gone-bankrupt-in-one-map/

Red tape blues: Small businesses fret less about taxes than over-regulation. (2014, July 5). *Economist.* Retrieved from http://www.economist.com/news/united-states/21606293-small-businesses-fret-less-about-taxes-over-regulation-red-tape-blues

Rodriguez, R. (2015). California farmers wasting water or providing benefits? *The Fresno Bee.* Retrieved from http://www.fresnobee.com/news/business/ agriculture/ article24003010.html

Titcomb, J. (2014). Mark Zuckerberg is America's biggest philanthropist. *The Telegraph UK.* Retrieved from http://www.telegraph.co.uk/technology/ facebook/10545680/Mark-Zuckerberg-is-Americas-biggest-philanthropist.html

UNESCO. (2015). *Funding.* Retrieved from http://whc.unesco.org/en/funding/

UNESCO-IPDC. (2015). *Projects: How to submit a proposal.* UNESCO International Programme for the Development of Projects (IPDC). Retrieved from http://www.unesco.org/new/en/communication-and-information/intergovernmental-programmes/ipdc/projects/how-to-submit-a-project-proposal/

U.S. Department of the Treasury. (2015). Debt to the penny and who holds it. *TreasuryDirect.gov.* Retrieved from http://www.treasurydirect.gov/NP/debt/ current

WHAT GOES INSIDE A TYPICAL GRANT PROPOSAL?

Always the Same Dish but with Varied Ingredients

INTRODUCTION

If you think of grant proposal development as a cookie-cutter phenomenon, you would be both correct in certain respects and sadly mistaken in others. As we will discuss in this chapter, there are some basic ingredients that make for a viable grant proposal. However, there are so many variations to the form, that there is often much more leeway to the genre than many grant writers presume.

More success comes to grant writers who realize that they can capitalize on the basic ingredients of the required elements of each grant proposal. By adding tasty visual, discursive, tactile, or aural elements, successful grant writers are able to develop and write proposals for grants that are more appealing and offer unexpected satisfaction and even delight to their reviewers. Particularly for smaller grants in the arts and sciences, or for modest in scale, social science non-profit organizations, including spicier content into a grant, where permissible, can help one's grant stand apart from all the others.

First, consider the request for proposal (RFP), which is also sometimes referred to as the 'call for grant applications.' RFPs and 'calls for grant proposals' can be as rigid as poets' conforming narrowly to the prescribed lines of *haiku* or iambic pentameter. Grant writing or proposal writing is highly structured and well organized.

At the same time, many RFPs or calls for grant applications offer myriad avenues of expression, as well as loopholes, which savvy proposal writers know how to exploit. There are two basic ways that make proposals more appealing to reviewers. The first and foremost is the proposal's content, which we will discuss first. The proposal's content is the guts and skeleton of the grant to be written. Proposal content should hold up well to scrutiny, as the patient seeking a clean bill of health would hope for after a magnetic resonance imagery (MRI) scan report from a doctor. The innards of the grant proposal should be able to tempt the reviewer with qualities of coherence, consistency, and solidity.

The second, yet still important area to be considered in proposal development and writing is format, or what the actual proposal looks like after it has been written and is ready to be submitted. The formatting element is the skin and fur of the proposal animal, which can be dull, opaque and matted like an oil-spill soaked pelican, or it can be gleaming, bright, and eye catching like a wild cheetah's renowned fur pattern. Be the cheetah!

Both content and formatting work hand in hand to help achieve a successful proposal. While of course the content of the proposal needs to be substantive and should be prioritized over style, a sloppy delivery can undermine the character of the individual or the organization—or both— that is being represented. Thus style, which includes format, while seeming to be a superficial component of the proposal writing process, is truly an important aspect of most proposal development and, commonly, ultimate success in gaining grant awards.

Before we get to appearances, however, let us first turn to discussing what lies beneath stylistic and formatting aspects of typical grant proposals. The content of a proposal ought to ideally be weighty, well written, and thoroughly researched. What exactly goes into writing a grant proposal that invites its reviewers to deem it worthy of funding?

ELEMENTS OF A GRANT PROPOSAL

Content

The content of a grant proposal is the substance, that is, what subject area and promise of work to be done is about. The substance of every grant will generally be comprised of the same kinds of sections, which we will go over here below. Each of these content sections establishes your own and, if you are working as a team, your organisation's and colleagues' special set of skills and expertise that would lend well to accomplishing the task your grant proposal is promising to be able to do.

The content must be current, which requires extensive study and data gathering to find out what your competition has been up to, and what they might be doing next. It is your goal to be ahead of your competitors in arriving at the finish line. So, do your homework as to what is typically considered as being up to date in your field of research, study, teaching, service, or product delivery. Regardless of whatever it is you are proposing to get done, the content must be accurate, and it must be explained in a way that is as jargon-free as possible. The acid test of any well written grant is whether or not your own mother, or that friend from an exercise class who works in a totally different field from you, could read it and understand what it is you are promising to do.

Naming Each Part: The Art of Seductive Section Headings

Most RFPs will stipulate exactly what the grant agency would like you to call each of the sections, or parts, and sometimes sub-sections, in your grant. The typical sections that are in many grants proposals, but which may be called different names or titles or headings, involve offering the reader some kind of background about the issue or problem that will be addressed, along with information about who will do the proposed work, and why they are qualified to do the work, how long it will take, how much it will cost, and what will result from the tasks once they are done. Here below in Table 1 we see this same information conveyed, but with different names, and in a somewhat different order or prioritization, for the headings in two different types of grant proposals. In the left side column of the table, we see a National Institutes of Health (NIH) sampling of sections that are required within the grant proposal. On the right side column of the table, we see sections that are typically called for in arts, humanities, and social sciences kinds of grant proposals.

Table 1. Samples of grant proposal types with section titles[1]

National Institutes of Health (NIH)	*Humanities and social sciences*
Aims	Introduction
Background & Significance	Problem/Statement of Needs
Preliminary Results	Project Goals and Objectives
Research Method & Design	Methods
Schedule	Evaluation
Budget	Future Tasks (e.g., Funding or other
Resources	goals)
Summary	Budget
Figures	Appendix/Appendices
Literature Cited	

The content that will be presented in the grant proposals' various sections covers essentially the same categories of information for both kinds of grants, but content is called by different terms, and it may appear in different places or subsections within the grant proposal. When you are working on setting up the skeleton format and organization for the grant proposal, be sure to follow carefully the RFP or the grant call so that you use precisely the terms and order that the grant agency is asking for. Particularly for government grant awards, the fidelity to correct format and terminology can mean the difference between a grant that gets considered and one that is rejected from the moment it has been submitted, simply on the basis of it not having followed the formatting guidelines for sections and organization.

Some grant proposal calls or RFPs in the arts or humanities may be slightly more forgiving or open-ended in terms of allowing some leeway on content and in naming of sections and subsections of the grant proposal. Many smaller grants do not even ask for section headings. It would be a great lost opportunity not to give section titles even if they are allowed, albeit not specifically sought, by the grant agency. Section headings are the grant proposal writer's opportunity to seduce the grants reviewer into skipping ahead to an especially juicy section of the grant that he or she finds most interesting.

For instance, a grants review team may be comprised of a diverse group of people with different skills and expertise. Let's say there is a grant proposal review team comprised of someone with accounting and economic background, someone with an arts knowledge base, and someone who has direct experience with manufacturing. The competitor's grant proposal lacks headings, so all of these people on the review team will be equally miserable in having to wade through many pages to get to the specific section of the grant that interests him or her most. But the wise grant proposal writer has added in very apt, concise section headings, so that the grant proposal may be easily navigated through by the grants review team members. The person with accounting knowledge is most interested in the budget, so she flips to that page first, before reading anything else. The manufacturing expert is interested most in how the promised task of creating a prototype for a bloodless insulin tester for diabetics can be cheaply produced. The grants reviewer with the arts background is particularly interested in the section containing the narrative and images about the portability and attractiveness of the design of the case that will discreetly house the insulin level tester in a user's purse or briefcase, or, is it small enough to fit in someone's pocket? Having apt headings enables each of these reviewers to get directly to that part of the grant proposal in which they are most interested. If the RFP allows it, having apt section and subsection headings can be seductive in that it is a rhetorical device advancing your idea: having and using section headings aids in the persuasive packaging and projection of competence of the proposal as a whole. Moreover, creating and using fitting names for sections and subsections of the grant proposal also helps to make the grant reviewer's assessment work go more quickly, smoothly, and efficiently. It never hurts to make your grants reviewer's job faster and easier. Handy headings could help, if ever so slightly, to render your grant proposal more endearing than the one before or the next one being reviewed after.

In the end, a generally wise strategy is to follow to the letter what is requested in the grant agency's guidelines. If the grant guidelines specifically call for section headings, figures, tables, or appendices, then use them to your advantage. If the grant agency's guidelines are more flexible and open to interpretation, then take advantage of every aspect of formatting to reiterate your grant proposal's message of enthusiastic confidence in your capability to do both original and feasible work, and to complete that work on time and within a reasonable budget.

Eligibility

Read eligibility requirements carefully. Most grant guidelines will stipulate who is eligible to apply and who is not. Some grants stipulate that only post-doctoral candidates may apply for a grant. Some grants establish parameters that seek out citizens of the U.S. only, while other international granting agencies may open up grant applications to international students, scholars, or practitioners in a given field.

Watch for stated versus unstated eligibility criteria. What are stated criteria? These criteria entail aspects of demographics, such as citizenship, age, stage of career, membership in a professional organization, status as employed by a specific kind of employer or in a certain field. Still other eligibility criteria concern whether or not matching funds from your employer's organization or institution, or from some other funder, are a prerequisite to even be able to apply for a given grant in the first place. Usually the stated eligibility information is very clear and transparent. Stated criteria might allocate funds only for pre-tenured, early career academics. Other stated criteria might limit grant applications to mid-career, tenured faculty. Still other criteria will concern subject area, age, gender, and other variables.

Unstated eligibility criteria can be discovered by looking up the titles of successful grants that were awarded in previous years by the agency. Such lists of prior awarded grants are often available on the granting agency's web site, but may also be requested via email, and if it is the case of a federal agency, through a formal freedom of information act (FOIA) request. Particularly for proposing to do grant funded work that has some ideological or political ideas or actions involved, the eligibility may be unstated, but nonetheless obvious. For example, I once learned from my mistake of applying to the Dirksen foundation, a small but fiscally sound granting entity which honors the Senate career of Senator Dirksen. I had sought through my grant proposal to fund research into the progressive advocacy of Democratic Congresswoman Barbara Lee. In hindsight, it is amply clear: my grant application did not get funded by that organization because it did not meet the basic, albeit unstated, yet obvious eligibility constraint: Dirksen was a Republican, so it follows that many, if not most, of the grants that foundation would typically fund would be in support of conservative, Republican causes, politics, and beliefs.

Fortunately, as we will observe throughout this book, initial failure in grant proposal writing is not any obstacle to successful grant writing. Quite the opposite. Learn from failure. Build on the comments and feedback that many grant agencies offer, either directly or indirectly. The most successful grant proposal writers have a sense of humour about themselves and their imperfections.

There is little room for ego in this genre of writing, which requires continually being reminded of, and working to repair or overcome, one's mistakes. As Snyder and Le Poire (2002) underscore, "persistence" is a necessary trait of successful grant proposal writers (p. 331). "Be tenacious," they advise, and "do not let fear of failure stop you from resubmitting a grant" (Snyder & Le Poire, p. 331). The corollary to that tenacity and persistence in continuing to revise and resubmit grant applications that may have been rejected is the need to exercise a judicious "lack of ego-involvement in the revision process" (Snyder & Le Poire, p. 331). There is nothing more humbling than rejection. Use humility to your advantage. Take that experience, and particularly any input, either directly or indirectly, that you can obtain from the grant agency about the shortcomings of the failed grant application, and use that knowledge as a basis for and means to revise and enhance your proposal for another submission the next time around, either at that same agency, or at a different venue.

After the failure with the Dirksen grant proposal application, I simply took and built upon that same grant narrative to study Congresswoman Barbara Lee's progressive discourses and politics. After further research, revising and polishing, I sent the now weightier and updated grant proposal to another grant agency; this next time I sent it to the distinguished Waterhouse Family Institute (WFI) of Villanova University, which supports research into socially progressive, ethical communication. Happily, the WFI grant was then successful: the grant was awarded, and my proposed research was fully funded.

I went on to study the oratory and leadership of the one courageous, amazing Congresswoman who stood against the tide of group-think in the wake of 9/11; she was the only 'nay' vote in congress (which voted 420 to one) on Congress's resolution on 14 September 2001 as the Authorization to Use Military Force (AUMF), which unleashed a perpetual state of War on Terror, and what today is a largely bipartisan consensus about botched forays into Afghanistan and Iraq, and uses of torture that contravene internationally agreed upon treaties and standards of human rights. In the end, Congresswoman Barbara Lee's sage, ethical voice was the same: she advocated restraint in expending lives, and opposition to spending federal money for open-ended conflict engagement, but the two grant agencies reading my grant narrative looked upon her perspectives on the issue of violent military engagement very differently.

Abstract or Executive Summary: Right, Tight and Full of Insight

The abstract or executive summary is usually anywhere from one paragraph long to one page long at most. It is short, vivid and clear. It explains the gist of what the proposed project is, who will do the project, why they are qualified, how long the project will take, and how much money is being requested to support the work of the project.

The executive summary or abstract is also sometimes referred to as the 'one-minute elevator speech' or as fascinating 'cocktail party' banter (Snyder & Le Poire, 2002). With brevity and wit, your pitch should reflect "sparkle value," it should show that your ideas or your actions are both smart and "counterintuitive" (Snyder & Le Poire, 2002, p. 328). Whether thinking of how you'd briefly pitch your project in a short elevator ride, or at a minute-long, chance meeting with a busy VIP at a cocktail gathering, these venues are apt comparisons because the time of decision-makers and people in charge is increasingly compressed. In a world where everyone's time, including grant reviewers, is impinged upon by gadgets like cell phones and iPads, the chance to tell your story in an impactful, energetic, and meaningful way is ever more crucial to the success or failure of your grant proposal.

What is your 'hook'? How will you capture the imagination and the attention of your reading audience, which is often a tired, possibly grumpy, overworked grants reviewer. What is the novelty of your idea? What makes your idea so new or different in its conception or in its application? What makes your project feasible or practical? What will ensure that you will get all of the things done that you promise to do within the time constraints of the project, which can be anywhere from one academic semester to one calendar year, on up to three years or more for larger, multi-party or team-based grants. What ensures that your budget is sufficiently modest, and that it is fair and parsimonious right down to the last penny? All of these diversified aspects of the grant must be condensed like a bushel of strawberries, boiled down into one single jar of thick, rich, sweet jam. The grants reviewer must be made, metaphorically speaking, to salivate: through the executive summary or abstract, she must be invited to take the first bite!

Narrative: What's Your Story?

Narrative simply means story. What is your story? Depending on the field of work or study, and on things like the type of granting agency to which your proposal is being submitted, the narrative can also be called by other terms, such as the 'discussion' or the 'problem statement,' among others. Whatever it is called, it remains your chance to tell your own, unique story that will, ideally, endear you and your work to your grant agency.

The narrative of the grant is the place where grant writers have the opportunity to describe in vivid detail what makes their project better or smarter than the projects of their competitors. What will your grant do? How and why is the work you propose unique and compelling? The narrative is your opportunity to distinguish your proposed project from so many others. By using content-based rhetorical flourishes, a narrative can help make a usually boring, dry genre of writing come to life.

Rhetoric makes the difference between a ho-hum proposal narrative that sounds to readers like an air conditioner's bland whirring versus a rich, descriptive, evocative proposal narrative that pierces through like Maria Callas singing arias by Puccini.

Rationale. The rationale simply explains what kind of work you are proposing to accomplish, and a compelling reason why the grant agency should select you, or your team, of all the people who might also be in competition with you to do such work. The rationale, much like the entire grant proposal itself, should be short and direct. Use clear, concise, short sentences (Porter, 2007). In terms of style, think Ernest Hemingway or Emily Dickenson, rather than the long-winded, overblown, minutely descriptive sentences of Charles Dickens.

The rationale must explain in a concise way what makes you unique? Why is your own or your team's perspectives, standpoints, and skills sets unlike most of the competition? Are you older, wiser? Or are you younger, brasher, and more able to think in new ways that will advance your field? What makes your approach or method different and more capable or insightful than that of your competitors? The rationale must briefly and vigorously set the tone that you are the one person or team that can get the work done on time and under budget, while also being innovative and making contributions within and beyond the proposed project's domain.

Positioning of project with peers' work. Typically most RFPs will ask you to provide an account of what kind of work has already been done in the area you are proposing to conduct work, and how your work fits into that larger context. Sometimes this section will be referred to as the 'Background.' For the purposes of this chapter, just know that this section requires that you do a great deal of sleuthing to find out what kind of work has already been done, and where the gaps are in that work that your own, timely and necessary work will fill in. We will talk more about context a bit later in Chapter 3.

Time schedule. The time schedule is simply a timeline of completion for the various milestones of the smaller aspects of the work you are proposing to do. Depending on the complexity of the grant work you are proposing to conduct, the schedule may be simple or more elaborate. Regardless of how many smaller, bite-sized chunks of work your project is promising to complete, it must be realistic.

Think conservatively. Consider all the other work obligations you will have during the grant timeframe. Life, family and work obligations, plus inevitable health issues like your own or a family member's bout with the flu, colds, fevers, or if you are traveling, common illnesses in-country that are typically listed on the State Department's traveller advisory section of each country. Even Harrison Ford was felled by dysentery in the filming of the original *Raiders of the Lost Ark* movie. It could happen to you, or to one of your project's team members, too. Budget extra time for such things; expect the unexpected.

Schedule your timeline realistically. Do not pretend you are super-human. Yes, there are some academics and other professionals who never sleep, or who seldom take time to eat, but the odds are you are not one of these people. The odds are also that even if you are one of those workaholics, the grants reviewer might not buy into believing that you are one. The grants reviewer will not look favourably upon a grant that promises to do three years of archival research when the RFP calls for funding only one year of work. So, carefully and realistically map out how long each phase of the proposed project would typically take, and even allow for a little bit of extra time to complete all the work. You will always need that time.

Deliverables and outcomes. The deliverables or outcomes section of the grant proposal simply discusses in general language exactly what physical, tangible things, or what intellectual property (IP), or what kind of actions, or what kind of combination of the three, your project will produce upon arriving at the end of the project's scheduled timeframe.

This section will answer basic questions of 'what' your grant work is all about, and what will be accomplished. Will you be coming up with a new kind of camera lens that will enable underwater divers to collect better visual images of whales in saline aquatic conditions? Will you be organizing a new consortium of providers of equine therapy for returning veterans of wars? Will you be theorizing a new or improved means for locating and funding undergraduate college students to pursue degrees in higher education? Regardless of whatever physical thing, action, idea, or combination of idea-thing-action you are promising to accomplish, it must be feasible. You must explain exactly how you can get this work done, and enthusiastically discuss the benefits, directly and indirectly, to the grants reviewer.

Budget

The budget should be as simple as possible. Be sure to carefully read the RFP to see what kinds of costs are allowable, and what kinds of things the granting agency will not pay for.

It is crucial to check to see what sorts of items are permissible and what are not. While private grant agencies may allow for some leeway in some cases, it is best to check with the contact person in advance if there is any doubt in your mind, or better still, to get permission in writing via email, for any such allowances. If you are working on a state or federal grant proposal, typically the grant agency will be much more stringent about what is and what is not allowed. Some agencies frown upon and thus do not permit expenses such as travel, meals, or materials. Other agencies might allow for only covering personnel costs, such as research assistance, but not costs such as equipment, like software or laptops. Scientific grants may, however, allow for equipment costs. Check the RFP for such details very carefully!

There are direct and indirect costs. The first kind of cost, the direct cost, is probably the most obvious kind of thing that needs to be paid for from grant monies. Direct costs are typically essential, specific items like fabric for a fashion designer, or hours of staff labor needed to get something done, like hiring a tailor to sew a dress:

> Direct costs are expenses that a company can easily connect to a specific "cost object," which may be a product, department or project. This includes items such as software, equipment, labor and raw materials. If your company develops software and needs specific pregenerated assets such as purchased frameworks or development applications, those are direct costs. (Arline, 2015)

The larger the enterprise you are working for, typically the larger the proportion of costs will be associated with the grant. For instance, if you are an academic working within higher education, there will normally be costs that are associated with your institution, such as overhead. Overhead is an example of an 'indirect cost.' Overhead simply refers to the roof over your head, or office-related expenses. In other words, overhead is usually the portion of your home institution's cut, or take, of expenses that will be over and above the items in the grant you have proposed to buy, use, or in some way incur expenses through the reasonable conduct of your proposed work. Often a portion or percentage of the salaries and support staffing expenses of large state institutions, as indirect costs, will be deducted from your grant's monies by your organization, especially if you work for a large entity. Indirect costs can be thought of as operational kinds of expenditures:

> The materials and supplies needed for the company's day-to-day operations are examples of indirect costs. These include items such as cleaning supplies, utilities, office equipment rental, desktop computers and cell phones... Other common indirect costs include advertising and marketing, communication, "fringe benefits" such as an employee gym, and accounting and payroll services. (Arline, 2015)

A general rule for estimating budget items on the grant has to do with the size and complexity of your proposed grant. In general, the larger the grant amount, and the larger the number of people or team members on your grant, the more complicated the budget will be. Will there be fixed costs? Or variable costs? Therefore, when you are crafting a budget for the conduct of work you are proposing to accomplish, particularly in a large institutional setting, it would be wise to work with others in your unit who have experience in estimating budget items. Larger institutions typically have one or more staffers who are dedicated to assisting people working on grants with estimating and working out the details of the spreadsheet listing of expenses on every grant. Seek out their advice and input early on in the proposal development phase so that you will be working within your affiliated institution's budgetary constraints and meeting their needs, as well as being sure to follow to the letter the items that are or are not permitted from the granting agency.

Another aspect that can vary according to which type of agency you are working for and which type of organization you are seeking to obtain grant funding from is called 'per-diem,' which in Latin refers to costs incurred 'each day.' Per diem most often refers to the daily costs associated with having meals or coffee, tea or snacks while you are out of town doing the work you must do to achieve your granted project's objectives. Government and state per diem rates are easily located on the Web. Some grant agencies allow for per diem to be included, others do not. It all depends. And it varies widely. That is yet another reason why it is absolutely imperative that you carefully read through the RFP or grant call to see what kinds of expenses are allowable and which kinds of expenses are not.

If the project you are proposing is a one-person proposal comprised only of you, then the budget should likely involve less complexity. If you are working alone, or with just one other person, such as a research assistant or colleague, your grant proposal writing and development of a budget will be much easier to accomplish.

While large granting agencies with abundant amounts of money to disburse might make it tempting to overinflate the budget, it is wise to resist that temptation. A budget that is conservative, carefully accounts for all anticipated and reasonable expenses, is a budget that will usually pass muster.

On the other hand, a budget that exaggerates how much equipment or travel will cost, or does not follow stipulated per diem rates, will not be taken seriously by the grants reviewer. Even if all other aspects of your proposed grant work are strong, including the novelty of the idea, and the feasibility of the action you are proposing to accomplish, if the budget is deemed to be inflated unnecessarily, it can sometimes be the factor that gets your grant shifted from the 'finalist' batch of grant proposals to the rejection pile.

Here below in Table 2 is a sample budget of a small grant that includes travel and the purchase of equipment to conduct the work of the project. With the Web, it is easy to locate the cost of virtually anything, from airfare to hotel prices, to scientific equipment, and other goods and services that may be incurred in your proposed project. Again, it is essential to find fair, reasonable prices, and not to inflate or balloon your proposal's budget, lest it get rejected for being too greedy.

On the other hand, if you lowball the budget to such a bare bones extent, you may wind up being awarded the grant, but taking months of salary out of your own paycheck to pay off your Visa bill, which is also not advisable. Successful grant proposal writers take the path of reasonableness between the looming cliffs of too expensive to the one side, and too miserly to the other.

Table 2. Example of a budget: Budget for study on lunar rocks

Item	Cost
Airfare to Houston, TX	$489.00
3 days' lodging at $89/day	$267.00
Ultraviolent laser to examine moon rocks	$149.00
Polarizing microscope	$1,300.00[2]
TOTAL	$2,205.00

Satisfaction: Content that Invites a Contented Feeling

Do not let your grant proposal reviewer feel like Mick Jagger when he and the other members of the Rolling Stones penned and performed "I Can't Get No Satisfaction." The successful grant proposal writer delivers a satisfying substance, organization, and appearance to her proposed project. In short, the content of a proposal should follow the checklist that the RFP or grant call establishes.

The proposal should satisfy the needs of the grant agency. The satisfying message is all about proper fit. Why does your proposed work fit better than anyone else's for this funder's organizational, political, financial, or other needs? The ideas, actions, tasks, and results should be discussed in a way that enables the grants reviewer to visualize your success, and to be satisfied by that success. There should be a sense of both direct and vicarious satisfaction through the end product of the grant proposal, once the project work has been completed.

Depending on the kind of grant agency is looking to fund project, there may be a range of needs to be satisfied, anywhere along the scale from pure self-interest to altruism. Variables in needs could entail marketing or visibility payoffs to the grant agency. Other variables could be innovative new products for manufacturing. Some agencies look for monetary rewards. As neoliberal discourses suggesting that virtually every kind of organization needs to be ever more entrepreneurial, discourses purveying self-reliance and self-sufficiency have become the norm in many areas of grant proposal writing (Pitman & Berman, 2009).

SUMMARY: THE GUTS OF GRANT PROPOSAL

To close this chapter's discussion of the key elements that go into a successful grant proposal, first return to the start. The RFP or the grants call itself will provide clues to the style, tone, word choice, and audience to whom you will be writing. The RFP or grants call will usually provide a fairly clear and stringent listing of each of the required sections of the proposal. Although most grant proposals must address the same things, the titles or headings for each section may be called different things, depending on the area of work being done, whether it is scientific or artsy, governmental or private sector.

The grant agency simply wants the basic, simple information that conveys with confidence the project will get done by a capable and reliable individual or team. The guts of your grant, expressed in both form and content, should demonstrate that you have the guts to get the proposed job done. Rhetoric conveying *ethos*, as credible character, is paramount to successful grant proposal writing: who is proposing to do the work of the project? What is your and your team's credibility? What kind of tasks will be accomplished? Do you have the guts to get these tasks done while also doing all of your other already demanding tasks as part of your everyday job? Are these tasks innovative, and do they represent novel, nonconforming ways of thinking that can produce benefits in the real world? How long will it take to get the work done? Is that a reasonable amount of time? How much will it cost to get this work done? What will be the payoffs? Is it too risky? Your proposal is the sustained, enthusiastic voice, telling your own, unique story, and answering each of these questions with confidence and expertise. The grant proposal's answers to these questions should show that you have done your homework, and that you understand your readers' needs. The proposal that is successful offers answers that promise that you of all people, are the brightest star in the constellation, that will shine light on the chosen issue or problem, moving it toward some kind of satisfying and tangible resolution.

NOTES

[1] Adapted from: The Grant Institute (2014). Advanced communication strategies: ICI persuasion and argumentation techniques. Retrieved from https://www.utexas.edu/cola/sociology/_files/pdfs/AdvComStratICI.pdf
[2] Thin sections of lunar rock are studied under the microscope (see Davidson, 2013).

REFERENCES

Arline, K. (2015). Direct costs vs. indirect costs: Understanding each. *Business News Daily: Small Business News and Inspiration.* Retrieved from http://www.businessnewsdaily.com/5498-direct-costs-indirect-costs.html

Atkinson, N. (2009). After 40 years moon rocks still revealing secrets. *UniverseToday.com.* Retrieved from http://www.universetoday.com/35404/after-40-years-moon-rocks-still-revealing-secrets/

Davidson, M. (2013). *Moon rocks under the microscope. Molecular expressions.* Tallahassee, FL: Florida State University. Retrieved from http://micro.magnet.fsu.edu/publications/pages/rocks.html

The Grant Institute. (2014). *Advanced communication strategies: ICI persuasion and argumentation techniques.* College of Liberal Arts, Department of Sociology, University of Texas, Austin, TX. Retrieved from https://www.utexas.edu/cola/sociology/_files/pdfs/AdvComStratICI.pdf

NASA Houston Space Center. (2015). *Visitors' great reviews earn Space Center Houston a top TripAdvisor® award* [Press release]. Retrieved from http://spacecenter.org/news-release-tripadvisor-2015/

Pitman, T., & Berman, J. E. (2009). Of what benefit and to whom? Linking Australian humanities research with its 'end users.' *Journal of Higher Education Policy and Management, 31*(4), 315–326.

Porter, R. (2007). Why academics have a hard time writing good grant proposals. *The Journal of Research Administration, 38*(2), 37–43.

Snyder, L., & Le Poire, B. A. (2002). Writing your first successful grant application to conduct communication research. *Journal of Applied Communication Research, 30*(4), 321–333.

HOW CAN I MAKE MY GRANT PROPOSAL STAND OUT FROM ALL THE OTHERS?

Star Spangled Banter

INTRODUCTION

Grant writers must always keep in mind who is reading their work. And this may surprise you: it is actual human beings. Not robots, not simpletons, but people with stresses and responsibilities, feelings and opinions, and a diversified and individualized knowledge of the world around them. They will delight in being released from the prison of discipline-specific jargon, which unnecessarily bogs down many a grant proposal.

To set your grant apart, you must undertake the elusive task of working within discipline-specific constraints and expectations, while also creating a voice that clearly conveys your nonconformity of thought. There exists a world of simple, spare communication that pares down the message to its most basic parts. Not only in fields of study such as Communication, but in many other areas, the message in the grant must be one that conveys "a practical bent, linking scholarly concerns with real world problems and issues" (Snyder & Le Poire, 2002, p. 321). The practical and necessary nature of the work you are proposing to do must be made obvious in every section of the proposal, from the first word to the last.

Meanwhile, pulling the practicality wagon is the horse of ingenuity; your ability to get the proposed project done must only be outshone by the comparative novelty of the ideas being presented. Unfortunately, many researchers, and particularly "humanities scholars often struggle, or at least do not attempt, to define any explicit social, economic or cultural benefit of their research" (Pitman & Berman, 2009, p. 323). Take, for example, a proposal to conduct a research study on a treatment for a specific type of cancer. This is not to say, of course, that you will be the only person to grapple with and study cancer. Nothing could be further from the case, in fact, there may be many thousands of researchers worldwide who are working on cures or treatments for the millennia-old health bane that is cancer. But which type of cancer? And what type of intervention? And with what technology, new or old? For instance, perhaps an herbal remedy that has been used for centuries in the mountains of Macedonia helps to ease side effects of chemotherapy in a way that controlled substances, such as medical marijuana, do not—better still, this natural herb's side benefit is that it is not a controlled substance, it does not act in ways that inhibit motor coordination, which is a key drawback of stimulants or depressants. In short, here the grant proposal writer is emphasizing the use of something old, in this case an herbal tea, for a new application, to ease uncomfortable side effects of chemotherapy for cancer. The idea here is to present a novel approach or context that has not been attempted before in addressing the problem of cancer.

FEASIBLY NONCONFORMIST

The Paradox of Reasonable Risk

The most convincing grant proposals answer the question that lurks in the grant reviewer's mind: How risky would it be to fund this project? How bold yet feasible are the ideas and actions being proposed? Persuasive grant proposal writing must comfort the reader into feeling assured the project is reasonable, and that it can in fact get done. On the other hand, the ideas and actions being proposed must appear to be original, nonconformist, and fresh. To ensure that the proposed project exudes that paradoxical 'feasible-nonconformity' means that you as the grant proposal writer are putting together concepts in ways that are both novel and common-sense. It is your task as the grant proposal writer to create the voice speaking confidently to your grant reviewer in a way that seems like it is an intimate conversation conveying exciting secrets. The most important question that is implied, and which must be answered with every sentence of the proposal's narrative, is 'why has this thing/idea/action not been attempted before?'

Inherent to the message of the grant is that although your idea presents a risk, it also presents an even greater siren's call to invest in the project. One side of the grant proposal coin is risk, but the other is reward. Of course, all grant reviewers worth their salt are substantively invested in risk-assessment to see if your proposed project appears to be meritorious. At the same time, the grant reviewer's task is to gauge that risk against the potential for reward. Reward is established rhetorically through your confident tone and through the carefully articulated and demonstrated list of established skills as the collective set of talents of the proposed individual or team that will get the hypothesized work done.

HOW TO SET APART YOUR GRANT PROPOSAL FROM THE REST

Context

The context of the grant is an important consideration, in terms of the project's substance and in its saleability. What is going on in the world at this moment? How do events happening out in the world impact the proposed project's work, if at all? How does the proposed work to be done influence particular constituents in the real world? What makes the issue your proposed grant undertakes trendy, timely, or timeless? Even better, what makes your proposed project appear to consider and grapple productively with all of the above questions?

Appropriate references to contextual opportunities and constraints may be introduced throughout the grant narrative. Geography or the application of place is one such consideration of context. For example, if a scholar is proposing to travel to the Vatican to study a brand new Pope's ability to connect with the masses of the faithful, that would be problematic in a context in which the Pope were to travel to the grant proposal writer's city in her nation; such a grant would be deemed less favourably by the grant reviewers because there would be less need to go directly to the Vatican if the Pope, in effect, brought the Vatican to the researcher's own locale.

Similarly, if a grant proposal were suggesting to research and analyse a television series' portrayal of acts of stalking against female victims, and that research required traveling to a specific television library compendium of such broadcast recordings, the context of the arrival of home-access to great numbers of television programs via new technologies and their purveyors, such as Netflix or Amazon, would render the need for on-site travel less necessary. Such is the problem and opportunity presented by considerations of context in the construction and pitching of a grant's rationale.

Conversely, context that is highlighted in successful grants accentuates the ways that the project is called for by unfolding events in the world. The problem of addressing the needs of refugees might seem pedantic or academic in times of relative peace in a given region that is proposed to be studied, yet in times of sudden conflict or escalation of war that affects civilians and non-combatants, the issue of large-scale human migration is rendered into a more serious and urgent concern. Context when engaged with correctly by the grant proposal writer, brings the concerns that might otherwise be ignored by the grants reviewer into quick focus. Perhaps the grants reviewer might expect his taxes to increase, in tandem with the governmental expenditures for policing, feeding, transporting, housing, and providing documentation for the migrants. An insightful grants reviewer will create the images that

31

bring the migrant, symbolically if not in person, to the very doorstep of the grants reviewer, asking for help.

Competition: Positioning of Project with Peers' Work

Successful grant proposals are able to demonstrate that your credibility, your (and, where applicable, your organization's) history of reliability and innovation rises above that of your competition. Yes, it is generally accurate to state that some grant agencies are snobbish and only fund grant proposals from highfalutin' people in Ivy League schools, or from first tier think tanks whose representatives appear as pundits on the evening news. However, many grant agencies actually would like to diversify their portfolios of grant awards to small, scrappy, but dedicated individuals and groups from less famous organizations. Are you, your team, or is your project, or organization, multicultural or bilingual? What about international? Then if you are applying to a grant agency that may promote intercultural or international exchange in some way, then say so: your unique perspective can enrich your proposed project's work in ways that your white-bread competitors, even the elite blue-bloods at institutions that really do have ivory-tower buildings instead of concrete cinderblock architecture, may not be able to do, much less to comprehend (Connor & Wagner, 1998). Everyone loves an underdog, so when and where it is advantageous, flaunt your underserved underdog status. Your proposed grant may only be ahead of the Ivy Leaguers if only by a nose, but at the end of the race, that is all that matters.

Find out what kinds of projects have been awarded in the recent past by the grant agency from which you or your team are seeking funding. As was mentioned in Chapter 2, lists of prior awarded grants are often available on the granting agency's web site, among other online repositories of grant award listings. The Web offers an ocean of helpful information, sample grant proposals, and models to follow for developing, writing, and submitting competitive grant proposals.

If you cannot find any such listing, you may also place a polite request to the agency via email or phone call to see if you may obtain a copy of full samples of prior awarded grants. Sometimes only lists of titles are available, which is nonetheless helpful in getting a sense of the type and tone and purpose of the recently awarded grants, in order to amend your project accordingly to fit the rhetorical and action-oriented aims of the grant agency.

Also, if you are looking for prior award information in the case of a federal agency, and such information is not readily accessible from libraries or online, you may always be able to request it through a formal freedom of information act (FOIA) request. Provided the information you are seeking is not classified, nor obviously ideologically contentious, surprisingly most FOIA requests are honoured, though it may take many months or longer to obtain the requested information. Do it, it is usually well worth the wait.

Other considerations will vary, depending on the field. In the sciences, for example, many grant proposals require what is called a 'letter of intent.' Also, strict formatting such as maximum number of pages or word count, cover page, signatures, and attachments must be followed lest your work be rejected on format grounds alone! We will cover more about things that can go wrong in planning and proposal development, but for now it is important to note that when a total number of pages or in some cases a total word count for a grant is listed, that number may or may not allow for the references and figures or figures that are listed within the proposal.

Still other considerations that may set your proposal apart from that of your peers hinge on points that you will need to make about your proposed project's merits, as well as its envisioned impacts, as summarized in Table 1 here below.

Last, it bears repeating, too, that if your employer has a dedicated grants group or staffer, get help from them in locating recent successful grant samples and related grants development information. Attend those grants workshops, particularly ones that are run by people in your discipline or field of work. And as always, librarians can also be quite helpful to you in finding grant proposal development information as well. Mentors in your field of work or study can also be wonderful sources of advice and tips. Seek out these people as your very own, Carnegie style 'Brain Trust' of grant proposal development support and wisdom.

Use of Imagery

As every memorable poet knows, using words that demonstrate ideas means conjuring up and delivering vivid pictures, colors, and shapes to one's reader. Let's say a grant writer may be working on a grant proposal to fund something related to health care, which may seem on the surface of things to be a rather antiseptic area of study. It is the grant writer's task to bring the images of health treatment into the mind of the grant reviewer. Take the true story of the woman doctor, Dr. Leslie Latterman, who was tired of lab coats that were designed for men wearing pants, rather than for women who wore pocketless dresses (Designs by Dr. Leslie, 2015). She clearly portrayed that women doctors and residents needed lab coats to have discreet pockets to hold personal things, such

Table 1. Mighty merit content[1]

Examples of intellectual might: Merit and related considerations of wider impact	
Significance:	How important is the proposed activity to advancing knowledge and understanding within its own field or across different fields?
Investigator(s):	How well-qualified is the proposer (individual or team) to conduct the project? (The reviewer may comment on the quality of prior work.)
Innovation:	To what extent does the proposed activity suggest and explore creative, original or potentially transformative concepts?
Approach:	How well-conceived and organized is the proposed activity?
Context/Environment:	Is there sufficient access to resources?
Integrated Research/ Learning:	How well does the activity advance discovery and understanding while promoting teaching, training, and learning?
Diversity:	How well does the activity broaden the participation of underrepresented groups (e.g., gender, ethnicity, disability, geographic, etc.)?
Improving Infrastructure:	To what extent will the activity enhance the infrastructure for research and education, such as facilities, instrumentation, networks, and partnerships? *Sharing Results:* Will the results be disseminated broadly to enhance scientific and technological understanding?
Benefits:	What may be the benefits (social, financial, environmental, etc.) of the proposed activity to society?

as tampons, unobtrusively. The image Dr. Leslie Latterman has conveyed was not only of the shapeless, impracticality of the traditional coat that was designed by men and for men, but also the image of the unfair and uncomfortable quality of that male accoutrement. Thus the image Latterman created was not just of the rumpled, dysfunctional vestment, but more importantly, the image was one of the desired and necessary alternative: a doctor's coat that was functional, fitting, and comfortable. In short, the women's doctor's coat would help, visually and substantively, to ensure a more equitable workplace for women health professionals. The tale of the arrival of women's doctor's coats is also the story of the power of images to make things happen.

Uses of Sounds

As every memorable poet and song-lyrics writer of 'ear-worms' understands, using onomotopaea, or alliteration, or simple repetition, can help to secure a cognitive hold over the memory of the already well overtaxed synapses firing in the brain of the grants reviewer. Just look at the heading above: "Uses of Sounds." That doesn't sound very poetic, does it? Perhaps not, but the seemingly ho-hum heading is using a stylistic literary device, alliteration. Alliteration is the repetition of the same, usually consonant, sound in a phrase. Now look again: "Uses of Sounds." In this phrase consisting of only three words, the 's' sound is repeated four times. In this surreptitious way, you, too, can make your grant more memorable. The less obvious these devices are, the better; when such sound-based ploys are flying under the radar, they can be just as effective.

Using such devices in a subtle way is important and helpful in making your grant proposal more memorable to the grants reviewer. The average grant proposal reviewer's memory of the grant project being proposed also needs to vie with remembering to bring the kids' soccer uniforms and cleats to their soccer practice after work; to stop at the grocery store on the way home and pick up cookies for the school bake-sale; and to drop off the mortgage check into the mailbox somewhere along the way. It is important to create both subtle and obvious sound bites that will cut through the competing messages clunking around in the cognitive processing of the brain of your grant proposal reviewer.

Uses of Media

Today's world abounds with endless assaults of multiple forms of media. We ride in a taxi, and in the back seat a tiny television proffers commercials selling soap, perfume, and jeans. We wait in line at the airport, and CNN or Fox News blares the day's news stories from specific ideological perspectives. Some grant guidelines, particularly for researchers or practitioners in the arts and humanities, may actually call for video clips.

Other grant guidelines, however, may only call for written grant materials to be submitted. If, as is often the case, the grant proposal writer only has words at his disposal, but needs to convey the cacophony of video imagery that surrounds people during much of their waking hours, the writer must offer active web site links, descriptive summaries, and screen capture images of those videos, documentary films, or other televised forms of media that need to be conveyed to the grants reviewer. By injecting synechdocally descriptors and images for actual videos or film segments, the live-action

35

movement and kinetic energy of the proposed project can more easily be looked up by the curious grants reviewer, or simply conjured and imagined.

Bucking or Following? Trends and Hot Topics

The level of risk attractiveness and risk aversion on the part of the reviewers at the grant agency will vary depending upon variables such as the agency's goals and the climate of acceptance for the topic or issue or problem being studied that is described in the grant proposal itself. In the art world, for example, depending on timing, risk can be deemed reasonable or excessive: determining the difference can be a question of timing. Recall Bjork's swan dress worn to the Oscars that was panned by fashion critics and was mystifying to average television viewers; today the outfit seems to be rather tame compared to the ever more theatrical get-ups of Lady Gaga. The grant selection and award process, like ephemeral fashion choices, is frequently based simply on fitting or poor timing.

If your grant proposal promises to follow a pre-existing trend, then your grants narrative must explain and demonstrate that your contribution to the trend of study or action is sufficiently warranted. Trend followers must still come up with novel approaches or perspectives on the trend itself. As long as that novelty in thought or application has not been accomplished yet as part of the present wave of work being done on that issue or problem, then your grant proposal narrative will be more compelling.

One of the obvious benefits of following a trend or hot topic is that there tends to be more interest in it, and, generally speaking, grant monies usually follow interests. The so-called hot topics can help grant seekers to garner grant funding (Snyder & Le Poire, 2002). Hot topics typically reflect interconnected social, cultural, and political trends in terms of ideology, while also relating to technological advances in terms of manufacturability and marketability, or user-friendliness. There is no doubt that topics which are in the daily news feed can often be helpful to the prospective grant proposal writer who is casting about for ideas to pursue that could be grant fundable.

However, hot topics can also become sources of irritation or possibly even outright rejection for jaded grants reviewers. Highly desired ideas or actions, or what rhetoric scholar Richard M. Weaver has coined 'God terms,' may sometimes transform, with time and new knowledge, into undesired things or ideas encapsulated by negative connotations, as 'devil terms.' Using leaded gasoline and asbestos in the 1960s were seen as exciting innovations among the hot trends of that era, what Weaver would identify as God-term-like as "science" and "progress." Leaded gas and asbestos were products as 'god terms' of their time; today these products are considered errors that have led to changes in the way gasoline is produced and sold (now mainly cars use unleaded gasoline) and asbestos is—and fortunately for the health of people's lungs—no longer the housing and building material of choice in the construction industry: asbestos is just another 'devil term.'

Today, a hot topic could include the study of ways to remove lead from paints on old houses, and methods to remove asbestos safely from older buildings. What will happen to all of the asbestos that is sent from demolished old buildings into the landfills of tomorrow? Does the Environmental Protection Agency (EPA), which was established under President Richard M. Nixon's administration, have any RFP's covering how to remediate the constellation of problems that formerly hot, god-like products, which have evolved into being seen as cold, devilish products, such as asbestos, will cause for years to come? Perhaps surprisingly, the massive nuclear power plant meltdowns in Chernobyl, Russia and at Fukushima Daiichi in the Futaba District of Japan, have not diminished the 'god-term' appeal of nuclear power, but that could always change; the trick of the perceptive grants proposal writer is to figure out when and for whom that will begin to shift, and to apply for grants according to those audiences and their timelines. Maybe some enterprising grant proposal writers are working on that very issue right now.

For some issues or problems, the characterization as a hot topic may be somewhat of a misnomer, since there are topics that are perennially and perpetually of vital concern to grant funders. Consider the replicability of the American institution of the military, beginning with the first general and president, George Washington, for whom the United States' capital city is named. During the First and Second World Wars, the U.S. military had the Department of War, which was later renamed the Department of Defense (DoD). The DoD was initially, and famously for its architecture, housed primarily at the Pentagon. Over time, of course, the DoD expanded to geographically take over a space outside the Pentagon, called Crystal City. After the terrible and tragic events of 9/11, the DoD at the Pentagon and Crystal City was deemed insufficient as bases of the military infrastructure. To grapple with the new and asymmetrical form of military engagement, the brand new Department of Homeland Security (DHS) was born, along with its associated geographic spot, near Tyson's Corner, in suburban Virginia. Tyson's Corner is just outside the capital beltway, and with the help of the rapid growth of DHS, new high-rise office buildings sprang up like giant mushrooms and filled with staffers busily working on this new, yet still longstanding, military hot topic. So as risk goes, across time, military related problems and topics will always be fascinating and generally will yield great potential in garnering grant funding. Just ask the grants proposal writing teams at firms like Lockheed Martin, Boeing, Honeywell, and Halliburton (Andreas, 2015).

Of course, if you seek grants related to the military, or to other reliably stable needs, for ideas as to avenues to pursue for grant funding, one need look no further than the classic Monopoly Game board. Issues related to jails and correctional facility maintenance, staffing and construction are generally grant fundable. The aging roads, bridges and sewers infrastructure is ailing and creaking here in the U.S., and, for international grants consideration, roads, bridges and sewers may be non-existent and would need to be built to begin with: perhaps your firm would propose to build them, and then do another proposal to maintain them. Likewise, the patchy educational system is ever in need of amelioration. Human health care issues, epidemiology, and public health problems and campaigns are likewise a fairly safe bet in terms of viability for garnering possible grant funding. Energy related industries such as gas and oil, and coal fired as well as nuclear generated electricity proffer still another range of possible lines to pursue for grant funding. Construction and housing represent yet another area of more or less stable issues that are continually addressed through grant proposal awards.

Most fields and industries experience boom and bust cycles. Therefore, the trick for successful grant proposal writers is to anticipate the boom when it is coming, apply for the grant during the boom season (which could last for mere months to some period of years or even decades), and complete the tasks for the grant funded project before the bust cycle appears.

Organization and Format as Persuasive Elements

Do not underestimate the persuasive power of the appearance of a grant proposal. Every aspect of the proposal writing and appearance should be as crisp, clean and correct as possible. The overall grant proposal should be aesthetically pleasing, and it should be easy to navigate through and to read. Study the basics of good print design. There are many books, web sites, workshops and short courses devoted to this topic. Study the principles of good design and learn them well. Effective grants writing requires knowledge of both writing itself, and also of the basics of beautiful visual design. If that is not possible, then bring onto the grant development team people who can do these things.

While good writing and design may sound easy to do, these are frequently very difficult things to achieve in combination, given that most grant proposal writing is done as one task among many under tight deadline circumstances. In many cases the grant proposal is finished in the wee hours of the night, when the grant proposal writer or team is thoroughly exhausted. As one proposal writer at a think tank I used to work for would say, "There's no greater productivity than at the last minute!"

The grant proposal itself, once finished, should meet and ideally exceed stylistic requirements, from using correct spelling (does the RFP call for British English, or American English?), to citing references according to the appropriate and required style guide. For social sciences, style guides vary, from the current edition of the official American Psychological Association (APA) guide, or using Chicago Manual of Style (CMS), or one of the many other guides that are field and industry specific. Should each section of the grant be numbered with Roman numerals or with Arabic numerals? Are standardized heading titles required, or should there be no headings at all?

In the old days, before word processing and online grant submissions became the norm, grant proposals had to be typed on typewriters and copied on copy machines, then manually bound, packaged, and shipped out by the postal mail or a shipping service. Today, for better and sometimes for worse, most grants are computer generated and submitted. Save any back-up copies you have as you go along because computers get viruses and crash, usually right at deadline time!

Even so, small aspects of grant proposal development may violate the expected criteria in organization and format. Depending on the grant agency, some violations of grant proposal norms may be viewed as acceptable. Typically scientific and many social science grant agencies have very stringent requirements and frown on, or even outright reject, grant proposals that do not follow precisely the format and organization that the RFP prescribes. Governmental agencies at the state, regional, national and international levels are usually the most rigorous in expectations for conforming to the RFP guidelines for how a grant proposal looks, right down to the acronyms that are permitted or not. From the font size to the size of paper margins allowed, to the color of the ink used, and so forth, these details must be followed precisely.

Many government and science-based grant guidelines contain a checklist that is required for the proposal writer or development team to complete to ensure that even the minutest detail is followed. Consult, use, and review these grant guidelines during every phase of the project development, writing, and definitely before submitting the grant proposal. Having multiple proof-readers to double-check that such aspects are met can be a very helpful way to catch minor errors that could potentially and unnecessarily derail a grant proposal award worth thousands or millions of dollars.

Yes, grant proposal writers should aim for perfection in spelling and formatting. However, the opposite case from strict guideline specifications can also exist. Some reasonable fluidity and flexibility can also be the case for formatting and organization of grant proposals. Smaller grant agencies that fund projects for individuals or small organizations are sometimes frustratingly vague about concrete aspects of grant style and format that they would like. If that is the case, try to get your hands on a copy of a prior awarded grant proposal, to see how that successful grant proposal writer handled the aspects of formatting or writing that seem to be eluding you.

When physical appearance and formatting aspects such as the allowable total number of pages, font size, or size of margins is not specified, then that can also be used as a persuasive tool to the proposal writer's advantage. For instance, are pictures allowed? Or are diagrams or pictures not permitted? If the grant guidelines do not say, then decide if using pictures would help or hinder your arguments and the overall appearance of the grant proposal. If images are not specifically forbidden, you may wish to sneak in a picture right on the cover page of the grant, since, after all, pictures can convey feelings and messages more aptly than words alone.

The size of the letters on the page, and the spacing between those letters, can constitute a reasonable loophole that smart proposal writers can exploit. Lack of specificity into font sizing or letter spacing sometimes allows for more discussion. More discussion or examples can serve as powerful means for increasing your proposal's ability to persuade. Standard font sizes can be played with somewhat, which allows you to say more than your competitors in the same allotment of space. Does the grant guideline say anything about 'kerning' (or 'mortising'), which is an old fashioned term for the spacing between letters—is the lettering spacing that is permitted tight, or is it loose? A tighter kerning allows the grants writer to fit in more words and sentences, more examples and other evidence, all of which can strengthen the project's viability.

In terms of gaining more space and time to press persuasively for your case, this is something like the equivalent of appearing in court, and the judge allowing you to speak for 20 minutes, while your adversary may only speak for 10 minutes. Use that extra time and space if you are given that gift of a vague RFP. Most RFPs and grant calls stipulate easily legible lettering, called font sizes, of 11 or 12 point, which was a criteria that was established back in the predominantly paper reading grants review era. Today, with the advent of many grant proposals being uploaded as word processed files and pdf files, words on the page can be enlarged on the grants reviewer's computer screen for ease of reading. Therefore, use this little bit of knowledge judiciously. For example, if the grant proposal must be submitted on paper to a more traditional venue, where the proposals may in fact still be read by the reviewers on paper, then it would not be advisable to use a headache inducing tiny font, such as 10 point font size or less.

However, if the RFP or grants call does not state any requirement about minimum or maximum font size, and if the grant is to be submitted through a web based online portal to a high-tech grant organization where it seems likely that your proposal will be read on computer screen, then you might want to consider taking the reasonable risk, and using the smaller 10 point font size so as to be able to squeeze in some more words through which to describe and convey the merits of your proposed project. What if your grant to fund a project to support better access for persons with mobility constraints or other disabilities will be converted into and read in Braille? If the grants review team is comprised in part or in whole of people with visual disabilities, considering sending in a podcast audio file of a reading of the grant—as long as it is not specifically forbidden in the grant guidelines, that could be something that your audience would appreciate. These are just a few among the many obvious and unobtrusive ways that additional flexibility in format, organization, and design may be incorporated into your grant proposal, giving your grant proposal submission the edge over that of your competitors.

Another aesthetic realm of manoeuvring is layout. The layout of the page refers to how much white space encircles the text that is printed on each page. The same concept of reasonable flexibility applies to stipulations about margins on the pages of your grant proposal. Back in the paper era, the rule of one-inch margins, and sometimes even more space on the left margin to allow for binding, was common. Today, with most documents being submitted electronically, concern about and attention to the width of margins has decreased. So if the RFP or grants call does not specifically state the size of margins that must be used in developing the written grant, then that omission presents another possible opportunity for the astute grant proposal writer to narrow slightly the width of the page margins. By narrowing or decreasing the margins to a reasonable extent, the proposal writer is creating yet another means to have slightly more space, and, importantly, more words, through which she may extoll the virtues of the proposed project.

Audience Assessment: Analysing Who Will Read Your Grant Proposal

In many fields of research such as Business, Communication and Rhetorical Criticism, Marketing and Public Relations, and Sociology, scholars expend enormous amounts of time and energy into figuring out how to best reach a given audience. Millenials? Advertise on Spotify. Over age 65? Put the message in traditional print newspapers. It is helpful to pitch one's ideas, to sell one's products, and to convince people to do things like exercise and eat right to keep healthy by writing about it clearly. However, if the right message is written but not adapted to the audience for whom it is addressed, that sad, forlorn message will fall flat, ring hollow, or be an awkward sight.

An essential part of effective writing is doing some data gathering about the demographics of the grants reviewing individual or team, and on the organization as a whole. Sometimes that information is transparent and easy to figure out. If you are developing a grant proposal for a think tank whose web site lists a staff of only eight employees, and only two of those employees are listed as contact persons on the RFP, then it may be that those two named individuals would be your grants reviewers. Who are they? Where are they from? What kinds of things are on their resumes or, if academics, the scholastic equivalent of resumes, the *Curriculum Vitae* (*C.V.*s)?

Be your own private investigator, and try to find out as much as you can about these grants reviewing people, their likes, dislikes, age, race/ethnicity, language(s) spoken, hobbies, and so forth. With the advent of Google and of social media sites, you can sometimes look people up on the Web and find out a little bit about them. Any helpful information can be used to tailor to this person or group of people the wording, appearance, content, style, or any other discursive or symbolic aspects of your grant proposal.

What if there is no single point person nor any direct contact information given about the individual or team that will be reviewing your grant proposal? As noted earlier, the design and content of the grant agency's RFP or grants call for applications, its web site, and its mission and products will offer clues to what kind of audience to whom you need to adapt your grant proposal writing and other stylistic and aesthetic considerations.

At the same time, it is wise to bear in mind that grants reviewing is a highly subjective process. The people reviewing grants at the National Science Foundation (NSF) and at the National Endowment for the Humanities (NEH), are just people. It is easy to stereotype NSF folks as pocket-protector-wearing types, but they may just as easily wear faded jeans as the good people at the NEH, who may just as easy prefer designer duds to tie-dye. These grants reviewers are not monolithic; they are a diverse bunch of people who have quirks, pet peeves, and are subject to good and bad moods, just like the rest of us. Moreover, rhetorical critics are aware of the issue of 'polysemy,' meaning that different audiences may interpret the exact same message in many different ways. If multiple kinds of demographics or audiences are a possibility for the composition of the team that will review your grant, then the best adaptation tool is to strive for excellence. Good writing is always going to be more persuasive than weak writing in the grant narrative. Beautiful design will always trump sloppy, ugly design. Smart ideas have better chances of beating out dumb ones.

The unifying factor for all grant proposal reviewers is that they prefer to read well written, top notch ideas, which are well supported by the evidence provided, and which offer narratives that exude competence and enthusiasm. Creating the impression of promising the moon and stars is part of successful grant proposal writing—provided you are actually proposing to improve telescope design, and can deliver at minimum the 10 prototype telescopes on time and under budget.

SUMMARY: A SINGING, SOARING SCRIPT FOR SUCCESS

Several factors will usually contribute to distinguishing a successful grant proposal from one that ends up in the rejection batch. Successful grant proposals are well written, are checked once, twice, thrice for matching and meeting completely all the items that are requested in the grants call for applications or in the RFP. Successful grant proposals must speak the language of the grants reviewer, when possible using turns of phrase or discussion patterns that reflect the age, language, regionalisms, nationality, and tastes of the grants reviewing individual or team members. Better yet, successful grant proposals must be written with the appropriate style, which may mean writing with panache for one set of reviewers at one grant agency, and then taking and revising the exact same narrative to read simply and more humbly at another grants agency.

Whether used boldly or more subtly, there are a host of content, formatting, and stylistic strategies that the successful grants writer has at his or her disposal. Using sights or pictures, sounds or podcasts, lots of white space on the page or very little, will depend on what is stated and unstated as being allowable in the RFP or grants call. Using poetic and rhetorical flourishes more boldly or more unobtrusively will depend on the data gathering the grants developer has done about demographics and makeup of the grants reviewers at the grants agency.

Grant writing is about taking informed and reasonable guesses, which means using your data gathered in combination with your best instincts as to what will fall or fly at a given grants awarding venue. Regardless of the demographics of the grants review person or team, the successful grant writer knows when to work alone, and when to bring on team members who can strengthen the grant's vigor of writing, aesthetic appearance, substantiated content, or staffing credibility, and whatever else the RFP calls for. Because in the end, the best grant is the one that is not only written well, but it also fits the grant organization's goals and needs: it fits like a comfortable, familiar, favourite t-shirt or pair of shoes. Being well crafted, the best grant stands apart on its own merits.

NOTE

[1] Adapted from: NSF Chapter III: NSF Proposal Processing and Review.

REFERENCES

Andreas, J. (2015). *Addicted to war: Why the U.S. can't kick militarism.* Oakland, CA: AK Press.

Connor, U., & Wagner, L. (1998). Language use in grant proposals by nonprofits: Spanish and English. *New Directions for Philanthropic Fundraising, 22*, 59–73.

Latterman, L. (2015). *Dr. Leslie's story. Designs by Dr. Leslie.* Retrieved from http://designerlabcoats.com/dr-leslies-story.php

National Science Foundation. (2011). *Grant proposal guide.* NSF Chapter III: NSF proposal processing and review. Retrieved from http://www.nsf.gov/pubs/policydocs/pappguide/nsf11001/gpg_3.jsp

Pitman, T., & Berman J. E. (2009). Of what benefit and to whom? Linking Australian humanities research with its 'end users'. *Journal of Higher Education Policy and Management, 31*(4), 315–326.

Snyder, L., & Le Poire, B. (2002). Writing your first successful grant application to conduct communication research. *Journal of Applied Communication Research, 30*(4), 321–333.

Weaver, R. (1953). *The ethics of rhetoric.* South Bend, IN: Regnery/Gateway.

CHAPTER 4

HOW CAN I GET MY GRANT WRITTEN AND SUBMITTED ON TIME?

... Or What Ever Happened to Work/Life Balance?

INTRODUCTION

The process of grant proposal research, development, writing and submission is, generally speaking, quite time consuming. Given the deadlines-oriented nature of grant proposal writing, it can also be a fairly stressful enterprise. This chapter will offer some helpful tips and strategies for ways to assist in transforming the workload into smaller pieces, which will help you to get the work done more efficiently.

While it may not be possible to make grant development and writing 'easy,' *per se*, successful grant proposal writing is achievable, especially if you avail yourself of some handy strategies for dovetailing grants development efforts. Grant writing is indeed a burden, but, as we will discuss in this chapter, the load can be made somewhat lighter after you have a few grant applications completed and submitted.

Grantsmanship refers to the competitive nature, like sports, of grant proposal development, research, writing, and submission. In baseball, there is the pitcher's strategy of the spit-ball. In American football, there is the science of just how inflated the ball should be to conform to game rules and to optimize the quarterback's ball throw-ability and the running back's ball catch-ability. In horse racing, the high-end breeding, access to genetics expertise, and massive monetary input often gives an upper class-based edge to wealthy owners of genetically elite racing horses. Everyone in every field looks for ways to gain the winning edge.

Similarly, with grant proposal writing, as we will discuss, there are some ways to render the process more smooth and manageable. First, however, some basic, common sense as to what constitutes this competitive 'edge' goes a long way:

The art of "grantsmanship" will not turn mediocre science into a fundable grant proposal. But poor "grantsmanship" will, and often does, turn very good science into an unfundable grant proposal. Good writing will not save bad ideas, but bad writing can kill good ones. (Kraicer, 2015)

To write well, the grant proposal writer or collaborative team of writers first needs to have done a great deal of reading and research. To write well, writing needs to be done at all. It is remarkable how many talented people there are, who write much better, and who are much smarter than many of the people who win grant awards, but: these bright, talented people do not bother with the hassle of grant proposal writing. To win grants, you must pursue them. To win grants, you must write grant proposals, lots of them!

GRANTSWOMANSHIP

The Art and Science of Grantswomanship

Grantsmanship is a throwback term, harkening to an earlier era. Grantsmanship is a concept that conveys the Old Boys' networked world of powerful men in industry and in the sciences. Grantsmanship conjures the image of a dark, wood panelled room furnished with button seamed leather chairs, sat upon by cigar smoking, whiskey sipping, silver haired white men. Alas, yes, there is more than a grain of truth in this picture, particularly as numbers of women and minorities remain stagnant in many areas of the so called STEM fields (science, technology, engineering and mathematics). To think, in 2015, the very first and only woman faculty member to ever join my present employer's Physics Department, which has been around for decades, was recently hired and is now on-board.

On the other hand, there is reason to take heart. 'Grantswomanship' has arrived, and is a skills set that can be learned and used to create success for women researchers as well as men in the sciences and in other areas of research (Rivera, 2012). For example, women today comprise roughly half of all medical students studying to be doctors. Increasingly, more men are becoming nurses in the health care profession. In the American political system, women constitute twenty percent of the U.S. Congress; ten percent of all state Governors; twenty four percent of all states' legislatures; and thirteen percent of all Mayors in American cities (Community Commons, 2015). As modest as these gains may seem, it is important to remember that the vote for women in the U.S. was enabled by the 19th Amendment, which passed in 1919, and which at this writing is nearly 100 years ago. Women and minorities may be outnumbered in many fields that require strong grants writing skills, but the numbers of women and minorities that are in government and in academia are steady, and improving in some cases.

In the European Parliament, the pace of women's progress is better than it is States-side, with representation in the Euro-zone at about thirty seven percent (Molin, 2014). For those lucky women living in Sweden, governmental representation by women is closer to fifty percent! Things are changing. Obstacles remain, but women and minorities are making some headway from the boardroom to the surgery room to the laboratory, and beyond (Rivera, 2012). The same obstacles and opportunities that exist in other areas also correspond to developing and writing successful grant proposals. These grant proposals are being read in greater numbers by women and minorities grants reviewers, too.

These trends indicate that grants relating to causes and issues that are important to specific communities or people, like African Americans, *Latinas/os*, Asian Americans, Native Americans and Pacific Islanders and other underrepresented populations nationally and internationally, await proposals and funding. Many local, state, and federal grants calls and RFPs actively reward diversity and inclusivity by asking for, or in some cases mandating, matching or teaming up with diverse partners, such as a small, women-owned business, or a business whose ownership and employees are racial and/or ethnic minorities. Teaming up with co-cultural, national, and international insiders and expertise is often a useful strategy of grantswomanship. Teaming is especially apt for grants that call for intercultural knowledge and awareness, or aspects in the conduct of the grant tasks, such as bi- or tri-lingual translation for community constituents of grant funded research outcomes and other beneficial grant activities.

Practice: Or the Benefits of Trial and Error

Years ago, when I worked first as an editor and then as a full time grant proposal writer, I had only a Bachelor's degree in Humanities. That meant that I was a strong writer and researcher, and that I knew a lot about humanistic research, including subject areas such as history and language. But I knew very little about science and engineering. Yet I was a quick study. The more I read about the science of electromagnetic radiation (ER) hazards, which was nicknamed 'RadHaz,' the more it fascinated me, and the more I came to understand how it worked. I assisted in editing and ghost writing highly technical reports for incredibly smart engineers, who were experts in these areas. At another firm, I went on to learn a lot about the ins and outs of the construction management industry.

47

Through team work, I would help to write and edit the introductory, or more flowery background parts of proposals and reports, and the engineers would contribute their analytical, scientific, engineering or data processing components of the reports or proposals. The engineers would often produce their bits in mangled, choppy, albeit scientifically correct prose, which I would then take and revise, polish, and render into clean, tidy writing that made sense. It was an excruciatingly slow and painful, reiterative process, but together, with my writing abilities, and with their scientific smarts, we somehow got the proposals and reports done and sent out on time.

Teamwork, then, is one vital strategy in competitive grantsmanship that can help you to get your grant proposal written and submitted. Teamwork, or working in a small group, comes with some benefits and annoyances, the gist of which readers as aspiring successful grant proposal writers will be apprised in the following section.

Teamwork: Benefits and Irritations

The first consideration in grantsmanship and grantswomanship is that typically in the social sciences and in the so-called 'hard' sciences, such as mathematics or engineering, requests for proposals (RFPs) are frequently bigger in scope, and awards of grant monies are higher. These projects often entail more complicated and hierarchical tasks, which means that there is a need to work in teams. Teams often include research or lab assistants, principal investigators (PIs) or co-investigators (co-PIs), who are typically the team leaders and visionaries. Their supporting team-members, who usually get stuck doing the heavy lifting, grunt work, may be graduate students or lower level staffers. Although it is not fun being one of these minions of the PI or co-PIs, it is helpful to experience this level of work because it can give you insights into the grant proposal development and grant work completion process. We will discuss more about doing the actual work of the grant in Chapter 5, but for the present we will discuss the things that, given the same talent and equally exciting ideas, would normally help to give one grant proposal the edge over the other.

Excellent English skills. To write well, an effective grants proposal writer also usually needs to have high proficiency in English language skills. Therefore, as is all too often the case, even for many international grants, if the call for grants or the RFP is in the English language, and if it is destined for a primarily English-speaking set of grants reviewers, then the quality of writing in English should be at a very high standard.

What if you are a research scientist who has ingenious ideas, though your strengths lie not in writing, but in researching problems in, say, physics or mathematics? You can always team up with a writer with an advanced degree and expertise in English writing, to help you convey your scientific ideas more straightforwardly, with style, and with correct grammar. As the only semi-serious jest goes, for many an English major upon graduation the first job includes the phrase, "Would you like fries with that?" Turn these talented English writers away from the deep fryers and toward your grant proposal project. For better or worse, there is an abundance of well qualified English writers, editors, and proof-readers who would be delighted to get paid to assist in correcting and revising grammar, organization, and, with some experience, even the substantive content of grants narratives, which are often roughly hewn gems in need of some polishing. (A prosocial side benefit is that many parents would also be glad for these English whiz kids to earn some cash toward moving them out of the family home and into apartments of their own.)

Therefore, if English is a non-native language or the second language of the grants proposal writer, then he or she would be wise to hire, at minimum, a qualified copy editor. It is up to the technical editor or copy editor to check the grant application for excellence in language aspects, such as apt use of idioms, and correct grammar and spelling. But with training and experience, editors can increasingly take on writing content areas and assisting with the whole process. Many firms and organizations whose business models rely on the production and submittals of many grant proposals may have entire staffing teams comprised of technical writers and editors, word processing and graphics design, and other support staff. These dedicated staffers can help to do crucial tasks, which saves time. Their knowledge specialization and division of labor can help save time in the writing, assembling, proofreading and checking for style and conformity to the RFP requirements.

Mad science skills. Meanwhile, on the other side of the skills coin, the same is true for grantswomanship that requires both adept English writing experience and advanced science or computational skills. You may be the smartest and best writer in Anthropology, History, or Sociology who is proposing to do scientific or survey research, but if you cannot schematically and substantively convey how you will crunch the numbers resulting from that research to arrive at accurate statistical findings, then your grant will probably not go far. In that case, it would be advantageous to seek the assistance of, or partner up with, a colleague for whom math or the relevant science field is a breeze. Grantsmanship often involves working with others for a well-rounded team which presents a variety and diversity of necessary skills not only for the development of the grant itself, but also for the conduct and timely completion of the action items or tasks that your grant is proposing to do or to deliver.

Planning Ahead: The More the Many-er

An axiom of grant proposal staffing, and for the conduct of grant proposed work itself, is that with every additional person added to the staffing section of the grant, the longer it will take to get the grant proposal developed, researched, written, readied, and approved for submission. For every extra person officially named on the grant, or unofficially involved in the grant, the complexity and annoyances of grant development become redoubled.

More people simply causes additional paperwork, red tape, and, given the human proclivity toward making mistakes, more errors. Names will be misspelled. The grants office at your institution will not have your research contributor's social security number, and the grants staffer will assure you that this person, with whom you've been working for the past three years in the cubicle next to yours, does not exist in the main office computer database. The person whose resume or *curriculum vitae* you desperately need on the eve of a major holiday, which is when most grant proposal applications seem to be due, will be unreachable, having already left for a vacation in the Maldives. An already famous for being grumpy mid-level dean will balk at having to drop everything for one whole minute at 4:59 p.m. on a Friday in order to lend her signature to your approvals form, without which your grant proposal cannot be submitted.

Be aware that such aggravating occurrences are normal, routine, and to be expected in the process of developing and writing grant proposals. Writing and submitting grants is a pesky business. Plan for these kinds of problems, and envision that other, related complications, ones that you had never even dreamt of, in all likelihood will also occur.

Budget in extra time to get the grant proposal researched, developed, written, printed out, and signed off by the big wigs in charge of such things at your organization. For instance, find out if the grouchy dean or unit head will sign off in advance, having only read the Executive Summary, or an earlier draft of the proposal. Frontload as much as you can such end-of-project tasks, like having the signatures page already signed, completed, and ready for submitting ahead of time. Then, when the longer, more time-consuming task of completing the revisions toward the final version of the grant narrative is ready, you will not be sweating the load of facing down a cranky boss or worse, the boss of the boss of your boss.

If you are working with a team, and if each team member must contribute a portion of the research or development narrative in the grant proposal, including their resume or C.V., be sure that they have done so far ahead of the grant submittal deadline. If you or someone else will revise or copyedit the grant proposal narrative or discussion sections, be sure to give the original individual or team contributors a chance to go back and proofread their specific parts; that is a good way to make sure that the well-meaning copy editor did not accidentally change the meaning of something to be grammatically correct but technically incorrect, rendering the draft of the proposal nonsensical but syntactic, which is also another potential pitfall of the team writing and revising process.

Budget in extra time for iterations of revisions back and forth amongst the project's various contributors. If you envision that your team will need at least two run-throughs of revisions, plan for four. Also allow for extra time for the most important scientist or engineer to get the flu, or to unexpectedly leave for another job and need to be replaced at the eleventh hour the day before the grant proposal must be submitted. By having back-up plans, shadow staffers who can fill in, and thinking of as many contingencies as possible, you and your grants development team will be able to get the work done even if something unfortunate happens. Because the unexpected is to be expected, plan for it, or at least be able to adapt and be flexible to come up with stop-gap measures and other work-arounds for life's inevitable mishaps.

Walk Away for a Spell: Or the Benefits of Drawer Time

Another important strategy for grant proposal development and writing, especially when you are in charge, is to allow for time to walk away from the project and to forget about it for a while. For instance, if the grant proposal submission due date is on December 24th, then put the most frenzied research, development, and writing time in by July 4th. Then let the rough draft of the grant proposal rest comfortably on your organization's network 'cloud.' Also, in the event of a data breach or system crash, back up the rough draft onto a jump drive, and also print it out and stuff it in a file drawer. But get the early, formative draft written, copied, and filed, and then, to the extent possible, try to forget all about it.

Then, a few days, weeks, or months later, or however long away from the drafting process you can get, return to your work in progress. Read it anew.

It is amazing how many errors, or silly, obvious problems, omissions, or poorly worded statements you can find in a rough draft with the benefit of being fresh to it. By just giving yourself a breather, you may be your own best proof-reader. Also, with the elapse of time, you may have become better apprised of new research or fortuitous developments in your field that could strengthen the methods section or some other part of your grant proposal. By budgeting in the extra time to walk away from the proposal, then you may be better equipped to return to the project with renewed zeal, better information, or just the fresh pair of eyes that are needed to correct errors that had not been noticeable before. In brief, by taking some time away during the early development phase of the grant proposal, you may often gain some valuable time for the writing or submissions phase, which is always needed at the last minute!

Maintain a Variety of Versions of Your Story

Chapter 3 of this book covered the importance of gauging, assessing, and analysing the demographics of who will be reading the grant proposal that you are crafting. A corollary to that task is to find out the standard, expected language, or jargon, or methods and other aspects that each grant agency to which you submit your proposal has, and then adapt your work accordingly to fit their image. Which is to say, to be a successful grant proposal writer, usually you must alter slightly your own, or your team's, core story.

The core story or narrative may be conveyed not only through the discussion and methods and goals in the grant, but also in more innocuous places, such as resumes or C.V.s. Everything in the document, from the font to your narrative, ought to be adapted to that highly specific language, that pinpointed style, and the stated and unstated objectives of the grant agency, as stipulated in the RFP or in the grants call for applications. Everything the RFP or grants call does not specifically disbar means that you will have wiggle room. Use any and all allowable avenues to subtly or directly reiterate your own, your team's, or your organization's message. Malleability and adaptation are crucial skills in successful grant proposal writing.

Any replicable section of any grant can be adapted to fit better the needs of the grant agency. For example, maintain a variety of versions of your, and if you are working with a team, your team's, resumes or C.V.s and basic background and methods discussion components, which are called for in most typical grant applications. Then you can more quickly draw upon a ready-made cache of the kinds of narratives or sections of applications that typical grant agencies look for. This way you will have less revising to do, which cuts down on the amount of time needed for assembling the grant proposal draft as a whole. For instance, some kinds of grant agencies may be looking for detailed exposition, whereas others will want quick, schematic snapshots of information. You may need to have one version of your research program's narrative fully written out in great detail with plenty of supporting evidence; have a second version that is more succinct, and which offers summaries of products or deliverables or other information presented in tables or figures through charts or graphs that can convey a lot more information in a shorter amount of space on the page; then, for good measure, have a third version that is somewhere in between, with some written description and some tabulated and other information presented pictorially or schematically.

To figure out what kind of narrative is needed for which kind of granting agency may take some failures and experience, but the key is to keep using, refining, and reusing parts of your or your organisation's story, telling and retelling that story in different ways that are applicable to each of your different audiences and grants readers.

Dovetailing

Another effective strategy for saving time in the research, development, and writing phase of the grant application process is to dovetail your work efforts. For instance, if you are a researcher, use and recycle relevant parts of your research, literature reviews, and other data for research papers, conference presentations, and publications, but also simultaneously use the fruits of all that labour for grant applications. If you are a social worker, gather your non-profit organisation's marketing or community recruiting materials or workshop materials that your organisation already has in use, and adapt them in part or in whole as ready-made building blocks, and use them to apply for grant funding. If you are a manufacturer, use prior successful projects of your own, or even of other individuals or firms in a similar industry, geographic area, place, or time, such as patent application materials, and apply those precedents to create a compelling narrative for garnering funding to build or manufacture your next product.

Saving and recycling seemingly mundane, every day records, such as emails or press releases, is another useful shortcut that prevents having to start from scratch. Such piecemeal sound bites, in which parts or versions of your work is described, exemplified, validated, or extolled, can be funnelled into grant proposal applications.

SUMMARY: MAKING TIME FOR GRANTS

To review this chapter, the main idea is that grantsmanship and grantswomanship involves using techniques and strategies, such as time-saving short-cuts like breaking up larger portions of work into bite sized tasks or delegating specific parts of the workload to specialized team members. What Henry Ford did for the assembly line the adroit grants proposal writer does for grant development projects. Time is a rapidly consumed commodity when it comes to grants, so it is helpful to save time by having partners or support staff to work with, and pre-existing plans and routine documents already in place.

Grant proposal research, development, and writing is a time consuming process. However, with practice and through experience, you may gain and hone skills in multitasking. Not multitasking in the traditional sense, such as walking, talking on a phone simultaneously while sipping a cup of coffee or tea, but rather the kind of purposeful multitasking that means you are efficiently dividing up your time and resources to devote care and attention to the most challenging parts of the grant one by one. That way you will devote less time and resources to the parts which you may already have completed on file and that only need slight revision, rather than totally redoing something that only needs a new spin or different format.

Successful grant proposal writers use a pre-prepared archive of information and related data already contained in often overlooked places, like saved emails, marketing materials, or easily accessible website background summaries, and other resources for records. Such pre-existing information can then be adapted and revised to fit the style, content, goals, and purposes of the grant proposal you are developing at the moment; meanwhile, also save each version in development, which may yet prove to be useful for a new and different proposal at some point in the future. Using an archive of ready-made background information about your organization, or your research, or your product or service, and on any other replicable aspects that most grant calls and RFPs require, means that you will already have a head's start on assembling the sections of the grant proposal with the looming deadline.

Speaking of deadlines, one counterintuitive strategy of successful grant proposal writers is, at its early or midway point, to give the project a rest. Set the grant proposal aside and, if possible, focus on something else for a while. Then, once you return to it, you may be fresher, or new events or facts on the ground may change the way you articulate the merits or outcomes of your proposed project. With some time set aside, you may return to the draft in progress more objectively; time away often helps to render more astute your or your team's ability to ascertain shortcomings, or even just basic glitches like catching typos.

Also, if you are working with others, the members of your grant development team can divide up the tasks according to each person's specialization so as to become more efficient. The only problem with working with other people is that doing so may add more paperwork or other time-consuming elements to the project, as well as more challenges, such as personality clashes or scheduling conflicts. Things will go awry, but that does not mean that your grant cannot be submitted on time.

By planning for normal mishaps, and by being creative and adjusting to unexpected circumstances, the proposal can still be completed and uploaded to the grant agency's web site. Or, if the web site crashes when you are trying to upload it, as long as you budgeted in an extra day and are submitting it early, then you will have the time to submit it once the web platform is back up and running properly. After President Obama's historic health care plan passed, so many people were logging onto it at the same time that the government's web server crashed; if it happened to the president, it could happen to you, too. Files get lost. Try to save your work in progress in as many forms as possible backup copies in case of computer crashes, cloud hackings, or other electronic spying or malfeasances that exist today. People get sick or leave work unexpectedly, so make contingency plans for shadow staffing if someone on your grants team calls in sick, or other common personnel occurrences that are to be expected.

Grantsmanship and grantswomanship is less about upping your game than it is about being realistic. Be optimistic in your story and in demonstrating all you can about your project's prospects for productive outcomes, but be pessimistic when it comes to your suspicions about letting that flaky staffer be responsible for uploading the grant pdf file to the grant agency's website, even if you have to miss your child's soccer game or ballet recital; delegate minor things in the development phase, but do important jobs yourself, particularly at the end stage: at least it will get done. Successful grant proposal writers are realistic about how time consuming grant writing is, and they are efficient at breaking up the larger endeavour into smaller, accomplishable pieces or chunks. Focusing carefully on one thing at a time, and frontloading as much as possible of the detailed work or red tape like getting forms signed, will enable more room to breathe at the hour when the proposal is due to the grants agency.

REFERENCES

Community Commons. (2015). Percentage of women holding public office. *CommunityCommons.org*. Retrieved from http://www.communitycommons.org/wp-content/uploads/2014/12/percent-women-holding-public-office-graph1.png

Kraicer, J. (2015). Art of grantsmanship. *Human Frontier Science Program*. Retrieved from http://www.hfsp.org/funding/art-grantsmanship

Molin, A. (2014, September 13–14). Feminist party gains in Europe's model state for equality. *The Wall Street Journal* [weekend edition], A9.

Rivera, S. (2012). *Faculty seminar: Everything you wanted to know about grantswomanship but were afraid to ask*. The Flora Stone Mather Center for Women's Lab Management Series. Case Western Reserve University, Cleveland, OH. Retrieved from https://research.case.edu/ArchiveView.cfm?e=164

CHAPTER 5

YAAY, I WAS AWARDED THE GRANT, NOW WHAT?

The Art of the Progress Report

INTRODUCTION

Congratulations! You have just received the happy news that, after running the gauntlet of cantankerous grant reviewers, your grant proposal successfully passed muster, and your project has been awarded grant funding. You would be correct if you ever thought the process was difficult in researching, developing, writing, revising, proofreading, checking for conformity to the content and formatting guidelines of grants call or RFP, and waiting some weeks or months or possibly even up to a full year to hear any news of results. However gruelling the proposal process may have been in obtaining the grant award, said work usually pales in comparison to the work required to complete all of the promised tasks. The lassoing of the moon and netting of the stars, about which your grant narrative waxed poetic, must now be done. Once you have obtained the grant award, frequently there is even more work to do than ever. Be forewarned: no good grant award goes unpunished.

This chapter will discuss the view from the top of the grants mountain, having planted the flag of success in being a grant awardee. From up here, you have the beautiful panoramic view of all the leading work that you and, if working collaboratively, your team have finished: the rough drafts of the grant proposal behind you, the squabbles over points of contention, such as: who would get to be named as first author on the grant-funded research publications, or who gets to travel in winter to meet the VIP in the lush, tropical locale where your manufacturing plant is located, or which staffer at your non-profit will co-star with a celebrity in your grant funded public service announcement, or who will do the legwork of running the job-skills training workshop—inside the region's largest correctional facility? Yes, this is a moment to savour, a brief wisp of time in which to relish your success. It is also a time not to be wasted, for there is much to do!

After you have spent a few hours gloating, then it will be time to return to working at an even more frenzied pace, for, dear reader and grants proposal writer, there is as much, if not more, work to do once the grant has received an award of funding. This chapter will sketch out some strategies and suggestions for coping with the glorious problem of being a successful grant proposal writer. Having won the grant award means you must next deal with the copious paperwork of tracking the grant's progress, including handling all of the necessary forms and expense reports for following the grant's budget; writing progress reports on tasks that have been done to date; conducting the actual work that was promised within the grant proposal; sometimes asking for more time to finish certain tasks; and last, then writing the final or completion report, as well as any post-completion reports. This chapter explains and discusses some smart ways to manage and consolidate these responsibilities and tasks, rendering each function of the grant work more compartmentalized and achievable.

MARKETING AND PUBLIC RELATIONS FOR THE GRANT AWARD

A Word on Necessary Gloating or Polite Immodesty

Before we get to the nuts and bolts of how to do the work of the grant project and how to write successful progress reports and completion reports, we must address the display of emotion we just noted above, that of gloating. If you are in a competitive industry (and who isn't these days?), gloating, or immodesty has become a virtue. Indeed, gloating or making immodest statements, in the form of marketing and public relations, has become a means to continuing and furthering one's success. It sometimes takes having won a grant award to get another grant award, and the next, and the one after that.

If you have been lucky enough to win a grant award, do not lose a moment of time. Be sure that from your mountain peak of grant proposal writing success, that you use your largest, loudest alpenhorn to communicate to audiences which are essential to the conduct of your grant proposed work, and to people and organizations who may fund your next project. Think of all of your current project's constituents, as well as reviewers in peer grant agencies to whom you may yet apply for future grants. Also consider your most dreaded, formidable, imposing adversaries, who may very well be your competitors for future grant applications that you will undertake.

Then, once you have all of these people listed, contact them and gloat, which is to say, make them perfectly aware of your grant award, which advertises and enables them to ascertain that, in the game of grantswomanship or grantsmanship, you are a player. Let everyone hear the good news. Let them all know that you won. You are a winner, and your competitors and future grantors alike must be apprised of this and come to acknowledge it.

For your grant-getting adversaries, publically displaying your grant writing prowess may psych them out, eroding their edge, while sharpening your own. Politely and professionally reminding peers and competitors of your excellence is a good thing. Enemies may not like you, but they may respect you, or your line of work, or your methods, or ideas, just a little bit more. As a message for your potential future grant funders, horn-tooting may set prospective grant agencies' sights on you as a safe bet or rising star to fund in the near term.

This requisite marketing and public relations to convey news of your grant award may be done directly or indirectly. Your grant award public relations blitz can be done directly, through statements in industry or discipline specific media venues for informing people like peers or competitors of the award. Communicate briefly, politely and modestly through paper form, such as in mass mailings in postal mail, newspapers, paper posters, in-box flyers; and in electronic form, such as via emails, listservs, web-based newsletters, blogs, web sites, Twitter, Facebook. Also be sure to share the good news with colleagues and supervisors in person and by telephone.

Your grant award advertising may also be done for you indirectly, such as through announcements by the grant agency itself in channels such as print or electronic publications. Broadcast the news of your successes through the media apparatuses of national and international professional associations of which you are a member, and they will share the felicitous news. Last, but never least, be sure to tell the most gossipy person you know in your field, industry or organization about your grant award: the gossip will do this crucial marketing and PR work for you for free. Use whatever other means available to you of sharing the good news that you have won this grant. After you, your grant agency, or associates have done this professional form of gloating, as a purposeful marketing version of peacock feather spreading and strutting, then you must roll up your sleeves, or don your Madeleine Albright-styled giant power brooch, and get to work on the grant funded project itself.

PROGRESS REPORTS

A Turtle's Progress: Slow and Steady

After winning the award, there are essentially two, twin tracks of labour that the person or team in charge of the grant must now accomplish. There is the actual proposed grant labour, and there is the meta-labour of reporting on that labour. The one track of labour, the meta-labour, is the responsibility you have to the grant agency to *report on the progress being made toward*

59

achieving the goals or objectives you stated you would complete by the end of your grant award timeline. The other track of workload, the actual labour itself, which simultaneously must be done, is the specific phases of work necessary to do the job that was proposed, and which has now been awarded, for the grant project.

First let's examine the meta-labour, or the reporting aspect of the grant work. To be able to report on what is being done, while it may sound simple, things do need to get done. Sometimes in the day-to-day operation of a job, or in the running of an organization, it is easy to forget, or let fall to the bottom of the to-do list, the tasks that were promised in the grant proposal. It is imperative to keep that work going, if ever so slowly. Compel your project's turtle to move forward, one step at a time, even if each unfolding step may seem like a less urgent priority than the hundred other tasks that also need to be done as part of the job.

Keep the project on the radar screen of not just the grant proposal developer, but if you are working in a team, also on everyone's shared screen. Set up automatic reminders in a variety of forms, ranging from instant messaging pesterings to periodic emails; and never underestimate the power of an old fashioned, paper memo, written on actual paper, printed out, copied to the other relevant members of the grant team, and initialled with an ink pen. Slap post-it-note reminders on the computer screens of whomever is listed on the project. Put up a giant dry-erase calendar in the office or hallway where people will see it several times a day. If you are working in a team, set up periodic but brief meetings in person or through media like group Skype, asking for updates from the contributing team members about their progress so far. Whatever it takes to keep yourself and anyone else on track, do it.

Honey-Do's and Swag Bags.   Also, in the conduct and reporting phase of the awarded grant, remember your 'Honey-Do's.' In the South, where my family is from, expressing gratitude is a cultural habit. So that when you ask for a favour from someone, in addition to asking, "Honey, will you do this, or will you do that for me?" you will also provide some tangible incentive, such as baking a batch of home-made cookies for the person, maybe even before they have done what you requested of them. Small, thoughtful gestures show thanks and appreciation for their effort. In modern day managerial jargon, this expression of gratitude may be referred to as "incentivizing" or as a "swag bag," or if you are a Yankee city-slicker, a monetary "bonus" (the latter could be seen as anything from necessary to insulting, depending on the perspective of folks from other parts of the country or world).

Whatever you want to call it, and whatever fits best the region or place where you are doing your job, people like to feel appreciated. Thus when people comply and are forthcoming to you with their grant-related contributions, be sure to express to them how much you recognize their efforts. Can't bake? Then, *if* the grant award's fine print allows it (as sadly, many types of grants, such as government or non-profit awards, may specifically bar things like food or gifts, or set monetary caps on such items), buy a box of donuts. Or take someone out to lunch. Do not be extravagant, especially if that is prohibited by the stipulations of the grant award guidelines; simply make a polite, symbolic effort at concretizing your gratitude. Just think of something that your grants team would like. Particularly when some of the problems that typically arise in grant work do crop up (which we discussed back in Chapter 4), and you must call upon someone to provide extra or last-minute help with something, if you have through your 'Honey-Do's' already created in their mind the positive association with you and the grant, that may just be the difference between their willingness at crunch time to lend a hand or not.

Timekeeping: Scheduling, Rescheduling, and Stretching

Time management of grant proposal project work is always a challenge. At the start of the grant, it always seems like there is plenty of time, so the pace of getting smaller tasks done goes slowly. By the mid-point of the grant, which usually requires writing some kind of *mid-term progress report*, the sense of urgency in completing unfinished tasks becomes more pressing. By the end of the grant, there is often not enough time to finish every single thing that was promised, so there may be a need to file a *request for an extension* of time in which to complete the projected tasks.

Beyond *grant completion reports* or *outcomes reports*, sometimes grant agencies will allow for *post-project reporting* on any remaining tasks that were completed after the official timeframe that was approved in the original grant proposal. Leeway on issues of time varies wildly depending on the nature and purpose of the grant agency and the grant-funded project itself, so always read the fine print in the grants call, RFP, or associated instructions that may be distributed to you upon the announcement of the grant award. Today, much of this information is available in advance on most grant agencies' web sites, so be sure to familiarize yourself with the details from the outset of your grant award.

Typically grant awards call for the completion of the projected work within finite time spans. For instance, for grant awards in academia, the time span would normally be one academic quarter, or one semester at the shortest, and usually it is often one academic year, say from Fall 2016 to Fall 2017. For scientific grants, the award periods may be longer, because scientific experiments require scientific replicability, which is time consuming. Grant awards, whether in the public sector or in the private sector, may be one calendar year to two, three, or up to five calendar years, depending on the size and scope of the project that was proposed and awarded. Some grant funded projects are permitted to have project 'add-ons' or extensions, which may become necessary for big, complicated projects such as producing a new kind of commercial airplane, or for time- and labour-intensive projects such as filming and producing a hand-molded, clay animation ('claymation') movie.

What if you are nearing the middle, or are towards the end of the time span of your grant project, but you have more than half of the work left to do? There is simply not enough time to get all of the work done. While this unpleasant scenario should be avoided if at all possible, most grant agencies allow for unexpected obstacles to appear, and the agency may permit you to request, either formally or informally, an extension so that you or your team can complete all of the work that was promised. Imagine all of the contractors' construction and university research projects that were chugging along smoothly when Hurricane Katrina hit New Orleans in 2005, or Superstorm Sandy hit the greater metropolitan New York and New Jersey areas in 2012. Everyone in the grants world who was affected by these events would have had to file extensions, or possibly even make plans for project cancellations. What else can one do if the grant proposal called for historic renovations of a home that was washed clean from its foundations, and which was crushed by other moving debris into bits that floated away? Grant agencies and their staffers understand that unforeseen events can occur, and many formalized grant award guidelines have contingency reporting and related activities already discussed and explained, so read through them carefully upon receipt of the grant award. If such problems are not explicitly discussed in the grant award guidelines, or you are unsure of how to handle such requests for extensions should that case ever apply to your grant project, contact directly the grant agency's listed point person to find out what to do.

Budgeting: Use It or Lose It

Keep careful track of how much you and, if working in a team, your colleagues are spending from the grant awarded monies. As the grant proposal developer and writer, unless your organization is large enough to delegate budgeting to a dedicated staff accountant, it is often up to you to gather and maintain originals and copies of receipts for all manner of expenses, from coffee to copy machines, and clerical staff hours to widgets.

The grant award guidelines will state clearly what is allowable and what is not. If you are not sure whether a given expense is allowable or not, then contact your grant award's point person at the grant agency and ask. For small, arts and humanities grants, this kind of bean-counting may be less of an issue, but increasingly, given the many scandals over excesses or bribes and other problems related to contractors and other public employees spending of citizens' tax monies, when it comes to large sized monetary awards, it is better to err on the side of caution than to possibly face jail time.

Private grant agencies may be somewhat more flexible on the allocations of spending between categories, such as staff labour or equipment, whereas other grant funders, like local, state or federal government entities, may require that everything be spent down to the penny in exactly the category for which the cash was proposed to be allocated. Some grant agencies may ask for their money back if it has not all been spent, so be sure you are not hoarding the grant monies so much that there will be any left over at the end of the grant period. The goal is to not underspend, nor to overspend, but to spend the amount that matches as closely as possible what the grant agency awarded your project.

Be aware that in larger organizations, such as academic research institutions, that the organization you are working for during the conduct of the grant project may incur costs that will impinge on or suction from your grant's budgeted expenses in some way. Again, as we noted in Chapter 4, it is helpful and useful to discuss budgeting with your accounting and grants office staffers not just during the proposal writing phase, but also throughout the project conduct phase, to ensure everyone is in the information loop, and that no new events or processes will affect negatively your budget. Or, if any unforeseen institutional costs are incurred, find out from your supervisor or others with grants expertise if any matching funds might be made available.

Working on It: Follow the Phased Plan

The reporting on the conduct of work depends on and is tied to this second, yet even more vital, of the twin tracks of grant award funded labour, which is comprised of the tasks and workload that the grant proposed to do. Now that we have discussed the all-important work of documenting and reporting on each phase of the work of the grant, it is time to examine ways to accomplish the work of the grant itself.

After the grant award has been received, and once the project has been initiated, it is sometimes easy to forget everything that you promised to do. One of the best strategies for keeping on task is to return to your grant proposal's narrative, methods, timeline and other relevant sections for guidance. The grant proposal you have written is also your roadmap toward successful completion of the work. Return to your proposal to set the pace and to establish shorter deadlines for each phase that is part of the overall project. Subdivide into smaller parts and sub-tasks as much of the grant work as you can. Subdivision into small and discrete pieces the tasks of each phase of the overall project not only will help your turtle to keep moving forward, but it will also provide the added psychological benefit of serving as a confidence booster in your or your organization's capacity and reliability in getting the project done. In addition, doing the little bits, a little bit at a time, also provides fodder for talking points that are needed in progress reports.

If possible, design these shorter, smaller pieces of work to be linked with internal, unofficial deadlines. Such informal deadlines enable grant project managers to establish parameters for built-in accountability to people within or beyond your organization. Having informal promises to share parts of your grant-labour results will also create an added incentive for you, and, if working collaboratively, your team, to initiate and to complete many of the smaller steps toward the larger goals of the project.

Perhaps the proposed project work is conducting research, gathering and publishing data. Then you may want to propose to give an informal, brown-bag lunch presentation somewhere on campus or in the community at about the time in your planned project where you should have at least completed the writing for the review of research literature. Or, if the award was for a non-profit organization, you may wish to set up a meeting with the city council apprising council members of your plan to conduct activities that are beneficial to your community. For instance, if you have proposed and been grant funded to set up a no-kill animal shelter, then the smaller, phased parts of that project would entail activities such as: hiring qualified full time staffers, and training volunteers in the maintenance, cleaning, feeding, and best practices for caring for and locating temporary or permanent home-family matches for a large number of unwanted pets in your town. By meeting with people who will be affected by each of these steps, you must focus on and best of all finish, the smaller, more easily achieved tasks of your grant project. Combining networking opportunities such as this may also assist you in learning shortcuts, or finding allies in your area of work who may serve as wise mentors. By seeking to share your expertise and your project with like-minded professionals or constituents, you can increase your odds of receiving serendipitous support from those who may be able to provide assistance or guidance on key aspects of your project, while also garnering benefits of their own from being associated with your project's work.

What if you may be a small manufacturer who is under a grant contract award to produce fine, hand crafted products. That may involve a host of beneficiaries. Products may require skills retraining and using the large pool of unemployed but skilled labour in your city. Take, for instance, what the beautiful watches, bikes and leather goods firm, *Shinola,* has done in Detroit, Michigan, or what the small sewing and textiles company, *Alabama Chanin,* has done in Florence, Alabama. It is usually easier to get grant project work done when you get connected to the very people who will directly or indirectly experience benefits or successes, however modest those side-benefits might seem, from your project.

Whatever the tasks your now funded grant has promised to do, it is up to you or your team or organization to get that done, and not to spend too much time or money in the process.

Deliverables and Outcomes: More Marketing of Successes

Upon arriving at the point in time when your project's hour glass has run out of sand, you should have in hand the literal results of your hard work. In terms of final reporting to your grant agency, you must convey figuratively and persuasively that you have done all, or at least most, of the work that your grant proposal originally promised to do. The final report usually requires attachments or enclosures in the form of appendices; each appendix will contain measurable results, deliverable items, or other outcomes, such as products, publications, statistical or other evidence showing your project has made its mark on the community, town, city, state, region, nation, or world.

The final report is no less of a rhetorical document than the initial grant proposal was, so all of the persuasive strategies and tactics that apply to plugging your ideas or plans, which we discussed in Chapters 3 and 4 of this handbook, are equally important in writing for the concluding phase of the grant project (Connor & Mauranen, 1999; Feng & Shi, 2004). The final report must demonstrate to the grant agency's constituents, its board of trustees, and its other decision-makers, that you or your team have successfully done the work that you promised to do, and that you have done it carefully, productively, ethically, environmentally, with a diversified staff comprised of linguistically, ethnically, racially, sex and gender variegated persons who are highly qualified in all of the proposed project's skills bases (Seskinen & Silius, 2006).

Ideally, the final project report must convey through final account reports and charts and spreadsheets as well as clear explanations, that you have met the budget. Or, if necessary, and is often common with large, multiparty grants involving many people or layers of subcontractors and other organizations, the final report's budget discussion may need to include a clear accounting for where there may have been budget overruns, why such costs were exceeded, and a reasonable explanation as to how this final budget could have been worse had it not been for the heroic cost-savings measures instituted by you and your team and organization.

SUMMARY: PROGRESS, EXTENSIONS, AND DELIVERABLES

In short, this chapter has covered some central tips and strategies for advertising your grant award to your peers and to other potential future funders so that you can continue to write successful grant proposals which garner grant funding. The writing of the grant does not end with the award, but rather the proposal is the beginning of more writing. Grant awards entail planning of the most obsessive-compulsive nature. There will be mid-term and end of term project reports, and sometimes also post-project reports that describe in great detail everything that anyone working on the grant has produced, whether it is ephemeral intellectual property, such as theoretical or philosophical ideas or methods, or physical products, such as manufactured goods.

Throughout the conduct of the project, the two key aspects to constantly monitor are the timeline and the budget. Both of these resources must be measured and used carefully, and documented in every manner possible. And as important and essential as time and money are to a grant project, they are nothing without the people who are directly or indirectly involved in accomplishing the work of the grant. Demonstrate respect and care for anyone who is working on the grant. Also, take good care of yourself, too, as the grant's central writing resource, the grant proposal writer may be the glue that holds together the precariously towering building blocks of the project's many parts. Seek wise counsel from people in your field and physical community, who may offer advice or networking opportunities that may support the conduct of the work in the grant funded project. If such people are not helpful, they may at least be able to alert you to obstacles or challenges that you had not counted on during your optimistic grant writing phase, but which present difficulties to getting your planned tasks completed on time and under budget.

The final report for the grant proposed— and now with any luck, fully completed—project, is much like another proposal. Only instead of merely pitching the idea of the project, you are instead establishing and advancing the idea that the grant agency made a wise choice in selecting you and your project for the grant award. Just as with the original grant proposal itself, your final report must convey through evidence, words, tone and attached appurtenances, great confidence in whatever it was that you achieved.

The most successful grant proposal writers understand that writing persuasively is an art form. Some day in the not too distant future, advanced computer software programs may supersede human beings in our ability to communicate in writing human feelings like optimism, and to convey confidence that enables readers to envision that amazing things can be created with human ingenuity. If you are a full time grant proposal writer, or if grant proposals comprise a central part of your job or career, fear not, that day has not yet arrived.

It is up to you, a fleshy, mortal human, to write a persuasive, compelling, and well researched grant proposal. It is up to you to keep and maintain project records. It is up to you to stay on the planned schedule, or to alert the grant agency when things are falling behind. It is up to you to create and adhere to financial constraints of the project. It is up to you to get the hundreds or thousands of sub-tasks in a project delegated or done, which will enable the larger grant funded project to be achieved. Now equipped with the knowledge of this handbook, you, dear grant proposal writer, who is not a robot but rather a fallible but ameliorable person, should have great potential to succeed in your project funding and completion endeavours.

REFERENCES

Connor, U., & Mauranen, A. (1999). Linguistic analysis of grant proposals: European Union research grants. *English for Specific Purposes, 18*(1), 47–62.

Feng, H., & Shi, L. (2004). Genre analysis of research grant proposals. *LSP and Professional Communication, 4*(1), 8–30.

Keskinen, S., & Silius, H. (2006). New trends in research funding: Threat or opportunity for interdisciplinary gender research? *Nordic Journal of Women's Studies, 14*(2), 73–86.

ABOUT THE AUTHOR

Ellen W. Gorsevski has experience writing successful grant proposals in the private sector, where for many years she worked for think tanks and contracting firms, and in the public sector, where she presently works as a professor and researcher. She has served on both sides of the grants application and review process, as both a proposal writer and as a reviewer. She earned her doctorate at the Pennsylvania State University, and has taught at American state universities in the Northwest, in the Midwest, and in the South. Dr. Gorsevski researches and teaches about rhetoric, featuring political, social and environmental advocacy for peace and justice. Her articles have appeared in top ranked journals in the field of Communication, such as: *Quarterly Journal of Speech; Western Journal of Communication; Journal of Communication and Religion;* and *Environmental Communication.* Her other books include *Peaceful Persuasion: The Geopolitics of Nonviolent Rhetoric* (SUNY Press, 2004), and *Dangerous Women: The Rhetoric of the Women Nobel Peace Laureates* (Troubador Publishing, Ltd., 2014).

Printed in the United States
By Bookmasters